DATA SECURITY BREACHES

NOTIFICATION LAWS, LEGISLATION AND IDENTITY THEFT

AMERICAN POLITICAL, ECONOMIC, AND SECURITY ISSUES

Additional books in this series can be found on Nova's website
under the Series tab.

Additional E-books in this series can be found on Nova's website
under the E-book tab.

AMERICAN POLITICAL, ECONOMIC, AND SECURITY ISSUES

DATA SECURITY BREACHES

NOTIFICATION LAWS, LEGISLATION AND IDENTITY THEFT

PATRICIA DIAZ
AND
WILLIAM C. LONG
EDITORS

nova publishers

New York

Library of Congress Cataloging-in-Publication Data

ISBN: 978-1-62257-735-4

Published by Nova Science Publishers, Inc. † New York

CONTENTS

PREFACE

A data security breach occurs when there is a loss or theft of, or other unauthorized access to, sensitive personally identifiable information that could result in the potential compromise of the confidentiality or integrity of data. This book provides an overview of state security breach notification laws applicable to entities that collect, maintain, own, possess, or license personal information. This book describes information security and security breach notification requirements in the Office of Management and Budget's "Breach Notification Policy," the Health Insurance Portability and Accountability Act (HIPAA), the Health Information Technology for Economic and Clinical Health Act (HITECH), and the Gramm-Leach-Bliley Act (GLBA).

Chapter 1 - A data security breach occurs when there is a loss or theft of, or other unauthorized access to, sensitive personally identifiable information that could result in the potential compromise of the confidentiality or integrity of data. Forty-six states, the District of Columbia, Puerto Rico, and the Virgin Islands have laws requiring notification of security breaches involving personal information. Federal statutes, regulations, and a memorandum for federal departments and agencies require certain sectors (healthcare, financial, federal public sector, and the Department of Veterans Affairs) to implement information security programs and provide notification of security breaches of personal information. In response to such notification laws, over 2,676 data breaches and computer intrusions involving 535 million records containing sensitive personal information have been disclosed by data brokers, businesses, retailers, educational institutions, government and military agencies, healthcare providers, financial institutions, nonprofit organizations, utility companies, and Internet businesses. As a result, a significantly large number of individuals have received notices that their personally identifiable information has been improperly disclosed.

This chapter provides an overview of state security breach notification laws applicable to entities that collect, maintain, own, possess, or license personal information. The chapter describes information security and security breach notification requirements in the Office of Management and Budget's "Breach Notification Policy," the Health Insurance Portability and Accountability Act (HIPAA), the Health Information Technology for Economic and Clinical Health Act (HITECH), and the Gramm-Leach-Bliley Act (GLBA).

The Senate Judiciary Committee marked up three data security bills and reported the three bills with substitute amendments. See *Selected Federal Data Security Breach Legislation*, by Kathleen Ann Ruane. S. 1151 (Leahy), the Personal Data Privacy and Security Act of 2011, would apply to business entities to prevent and mitigate identity theft, ensure privacy, provide notice of security breaches, and enhance criminal penalties. It would provide law enforcement assistance and other protections against security breaches, fraudulent access, and misuse of personally identifiable information. S. 1408 (Feinstein), the Data Breach Notification Act of 2011, would require federal agencies and persons engaged in interstate commerce, in possession of data containing sensitive personally identifiable information, to disclose any breach of such information. S. 1535 (Blumenthal), the Personal Data Protection and Breach Accountability Act of 2011, would protect consumers by mitigating the vulnerability of personally identifiable information to theft through a security breach, provide notice and remedies to consumers, hold companies accountable for preventable breaches, facilitate the sharing of post-breach technical information, and enhance criminal and civil penalties and other protections against the unauthorized collection or use of personally identifiable information. The House Subcommittee on Commerce, Manufacturing and Trade marked up H.R. 2577 (Bono Mack), the SAFE Data Act, to protect consumers by requiring reasonable security policies and procedures to protect data containing personal information, and to provide for nationwide notice in the event of a security breach. Several subcommittee Democrats objected to the bill's definition of personal information, arguing that the description is limited and does not adequately protect consumers from identity theft. The House Commerce, Manufacturing and Trade Subcommittee approved H.R. 2577 by voice vote and the measure was referred to the full committee for consideration. H.R. 1707 (Rush) and H.R. 1841 (Stearns) were also introduced to protect consumers by requiring reasonable security policies and procedures to protect computerized data containing personal information and providing for nationwide notice in the event of a breach. Congress may address data security during its consideration of cybersecurity legislation.

Chapter 2 - The protection of data, particularly data that can be used to identify individuals, has become an issue of great concern to Congress. There is no comprehensive federal law governing the protection of data held by private actors. Only those entities covered by the Gramm-Leach-Bliley Act, 15 U.S.C. §§6801-6809, (certain financial institutions) and the Health Insurance Portability and Accountability Act (HIPAA), 42 U.S.C. §1320d *et seq.*, and amendments to HIPAA contained in the Health Information Technology for Economic and Clinical Health Act (HITECH Act), P.L. 111-5, (certain health care facilities) are required explicitly by federal law to report data breaches. If private companies have indicated in their privacy policies that they will notify individuals upon a suspected data breach, failure to provide such notification may be considered to be an unfair and deceptive trade practice under Section 5 of the Federal Trade Commission Act (FTC Act). However, the FTC does not explicitly require private actors in possession of data related to individuals to notify individuals or the federal government should a data breach occur.

Forty-six states, the District of Columbia, Puerto Rico, and the Virgin Islands have enacted laws requiring notification upon a data security breach involving personal information. However, these laws may vary in their application. They may only apply to certain entities or to certain data. Furthermore, companies maintaining stores of personal data may find it difficult to comply with the potentially different requirements of various state laws. A combination of a lack of a comprehensive federal law addressing security breaches involving personal data and the difficulty industry participants report in complying with various state laws has led Congress to propose a number of bills that would require private actors in possession of personal data to report breaches of that data. The Senate Judiciary Committee recently approved and reported three bills that would create federal standards for data breach notification: S. 1151, the Personal Data Privacy and Security Act of 2011 (Chairman Leahy); S. 1408, the Data Breach Notification Act of 2011 (Senator Feinstein); and S. 1535, the Personal Data Protection and Breach Accountability Act of 2011 (Senator Blumenthal). The bills have similar structures and elements. This chapter will analyze the bills, as reported out of the committee, discussing their similarities and differences.

Chapter 3 – This is the Statement of David Vladeck.

Chapter 4 – This is the Testimony of Eugene H. Spafford.

Chapter 5 - In the current fiscal environment, policymakers are increasingly concerned with securing the economic health of the United States—including combating those crimes that threaten to further undermine the nation's financial stability. Identity theft is one such crime. In 2010, about 8.1 million Americans were reportedly victims of identity fraud, and the average identity fraud victim incurred a mean of $631 in costs as a result of the fraud—the highest level since 2007. Identity theft is often committed to facilitate other crimes such as credit card fraud, document fraud, or employment fraud, which in turn can affect not only the nation's economy but its security. Consequently, in securing the nation and its economic health, policymakers are also tasked with reducing identity theft and its impact.

Identity theft has remained the dominant consumer fraud complaint to the Federal Trade Commission (FTC). Nevertheless, while the number of overall identity theft complaints generally increased between when the FTC began recording identity theft complaints in 2000 and 2008, the number of complaints decreased in both 2009 and 2010. Prosecutions of federal identity theft violations have followed a similar pattern. However, while the number of identity theft cases filed and the number of defendants convicted both decreased in FY2009 and FY2010 relative to FY2008, the numbers of *aggravated* identity theft cases filed and defendants convicted have continued to increase.

Congress continues to debate the federal government's role in (1) preventing identity theft and its related crimes, (2) mitigating the potential effects of identity theft after it occurs, and (3) providing the most effective tools to investigate and prosecute identity thieves. With respect to preventing identity theft, one issue concerning policymakers is the prevalence of personally identifiable information—and in particular, the prevalence of Social Security numbers (SSNs)—in both the private and public sectors. One policy option to reduce their prevalence may involve restricting the use of SSNs on government-issued documents such as Medicare identification cards. Another option could entail providing federal agencies with increased regulatory authority to curb the prevalence of SSN use in the private sector. In debating policies to mitigate the effects of identity theft, one option Congress may consider is whether to strengthen data breach notification requirements. Such requirements could affect the notification of relevant law enforcement authorities as well as any individuals whose personally identifiable information may be at risk from the breach. Congress may also be interested in assessing the true scope of data breaches, particularly involving government networks (e.g., S. 2105).

There have already been several legislative and administrative actions aimed at curtailing identity theft. Congress enacted legislation naming identity theft as a federal crime in 1998 (P.L. 105-318) and later provided for enhanced penalties for aggravated identity theft (P.L. 108-275). In April 2007, the President's Identity Theft Task Force issued recommendations to combat identity theft, including specific legislative recommendations to close identity theft-related gaps in the federal criminal statutes. In a further attempt to curb identity theft, Congress directed the FTC to issue an Identity Theft Red Flags Rule (effective December 31, 2010), requiring that creditors and financial institutions with specified account types develop and institute written identity theft prevention programs.

In: Data Security Breaches   ISBN: 978-1-62257-735-4
Editors: P. Diaz and W. C. Long   © 2013 Nova Science Publishers, Inc.

Chapter 1

DATA SECURITY BREACH NOTIFICATION LAWS*

Gina Stevens

SUMMARY

A data security breach occurs when there is a loss or theft of, or other unauthorized access to, sensitive personally identifiable information that could result in the potential compromise of the confidentiality or integrity of data. Forty-six states, the District of Columbia, Puerto Rico, and the Virgin Islands have laws requiring notification of security breaches involving personal information. Federal statutes, regulations, and a memorandum for federal departments and agencies require certain sectors (healthcare, financial, federal public sector, and the Department of Veterans Affairs) to implement information security programs and provide notification of security breaches of personal information. In response to such notification laws, over 2,676 data breaches and computer intrusions involving 535 million records containing sensitive personal information have been disclosed by data brokers, businesses, retailers, educational institutions, government and military agencies, healthcare providers, financial institutions, nonprofit organizations, utility companies, and Internet businesses. As a result, a significantly large number of individuals have received notices that their personally identifiable information has been improperly disclosed.

---

* This is an edited, reformatted and augmented version of Congressional Research Service, Publication No. R42475, dated April 10, 2012.

This chapter provides an overview of state security breach notification laws applicable to entities that collect, maintain, own, possess, or license personal information. The chapter describes information security and security breach notification requirements in the Office of Management and Budget's "Breach Notification Policy," the Health Insurance Portability and Accountability Act (HIPAA), the Health Information Technology for Economic and Clinical Health Act (HITECH), and the Gramm-Leach-Bliley Act (GLBA).

The Senate Judiciary Committee marked up three data security bills and reported the three bills with substitute amendments. See *Selected Federal Data Security Breach Legislation*, by Kathleen Ann Ruane. S. 1151 (Leahy), the Personal Data Privacy and Security Act of 2011, would apply to business entities to prevent and mitigate identity theft, ensure privacy, provide notice of security breaches, and enhance criminal penalties. It would provide law enforcement assistance and other protections against security breaches, fraudulent access, and misuse of personally identifiable information. S. 1408 (Feinstein), the Data Breach Notification Act of 2011, would require federal agencies and persons engaged in interstate commerce, in possession of data containing sensitive personally identifiable information, to disclose any breach of such information. S. 1535 (Blumenthal), the Personal Data Protection and Breach Accountability Act of 2011, would protect consumers by mitigating the vulnerability of personally identifiable information to theft through a security breach, provide notice and remedies to consumers, hold companies accountable for preventable breaches, facilitate the sharing of post-breach technical information, and enhance criminal and civil penalties and other protections against the unauthorized collection or use of personally identifiable information. The House Subcommittee on Commerce, Manufacturing and Trade marked up H.R. 2577 (Bono Mack), the SAFE Data Act, to protect consumers by requiring reasonable security policies and procedures to protect data containing personal information, and to provide for nationwide notice in the event of a security breach. Several subcommittee Democrats objected to the bill's definition of personal information, arguing that the description is limited and does not adequately protect consumers from identity theft. The House Commerce, Manufacturing and Trade Subcommittee approved H.R. 2577 by voice vote and the measure was referred to the full committee for consideration. H.R. 1707 (Rush) and H.R. 1841 (Stearns) were also introduced to protect consumers by requiring reasonable security policies and procedures to protect computerized data containing personal information and providing for nationwide notice in the event of a breach. Congress may address data security during its consideration of cybersecurity legislation.

DATA BREACHES

A data breach occurs when there is a loss or theft of, or other unauthorized access to, data containing sensitive personal information that results in the potential compromise of the confidentiality or integrity of data.

The first state data security breach notification law was enacted in California in 2002. In response to state security breach notification laws enacted thereafter in numerous jurisdictions, over 2,676 data breaches and computer intrusions have been disclosed by the nation's largest data brokers, businesses, retailers, educational institutions, government and military agencies, healthcare providers, financial institutions, nonprofit organizations, utility companies, and Internet businesses.[1]

A brief chronology of significant data breaches follows. In February 2005, the data broker ChoicePoint disclosed a security breach, as required by the California Security Breach Act, involving the personal information of 163,000 persons.[2] In 2006, the personal data of 26.5 million veterans was breached when a VA employee's hard drive was stolen from his home. In 2007, the retailer TJX Companies revealed that 46.2 million credit and debit cards may have been compromised during the breach of its computer network by unauthorized individuals.[3] In 2008, the Hannaford supermarket chain revealed that approximately 4 million debit and credit card numbers were compromised when Hannaford's computer systems were illegally accessed while the cards were being authorized for purchase.[4] In 2009, 130 million records from credit card processor Heartland Payment Systems Inc. of Princeton, N.J., were breached. Also, in 2009, personal information from Health Net on almost half a million Connecticut residents and 1.5 million patients nationally was breached.[5] In 2011, another breach of patient data occurred when data for 20,000 emergency room patients from Stanford Hospital in California was posted on a commercial website for nearly a year.[6] In January 2012, New York State Electric & Gas and Rochester Gas and Electric, subsidiaries of Iberdrola USA, sent notices to customers advising them of unauthorized access to customer data on the companies' customer information systems, which contained Social Security numbers, dates of birth, and financial institution account numbers.[7]

Data breaches are caused by computer hacking, malware, payment card fraud, employee insider breach, physical loss of non-electronic records and portable devices, and inadvertent exposure of confidential data on websites or in e-mail. Data breaches are expensive, time consuming, and can damage a company's reputation.[8] U.S. companies are reportedly reticent about buying cyber liability insurance even though data breaches have cost companies millions of dollars.[9] Data breaches involving sensitive personal information may also result in identity theft and financial crimes (e.g., credit card fraud, phone or utilities fraud, bank fraud, mortgage fraud, employment-related fraud, government documents or benefits fraud, loan fraud, and health-care fraud). Identity theft involves the misuse of any individually identifying information to commit a violation of federal or state law. With continued media reports of data security breaches, concerns about identity theft are widespread.[10]

Cloud computing[11] also poses particular data security challenges as illustrated by the 2011 Epsilon, Sony, and Amazon data breaches.[12] E-mail marketing company Epsilon announced in April 2011 that its databases had been hacked, compromising customer names and e-mail addresses for companies that outsource their marketing communications to Epsilon. E-mails concerning the breach from companies including Citibank, Chase, Capital One, Walgreens, Target, Best Buy, TiVo, TD Ameritrade, Verizon, and Ritz Carlton were sent after Epsilon announced the data breach.[13] About 2% of Epsilon's estimated 2,500 clients were affected by the attack, which amounted to millions of exposed records.

Sony announced that in April 2011 certain PlayStation Network and Qriocity service user account information was compromised in connection with an illegal and unauthorized intrusion into its network.[14]

The Amazon Web Services cloud computing platform, Amazon Elastic Compute Cloud (Amazon EC2), suffered a partial failure when one of Amazon's giant server farms (the northern Virginia data center—"US-East"), whose storage and processing facilities it rents to other companies, suffered a lengthy outage.[15] Customers whose information technology was hosted by Amazon EC2 were down. These included applications like Foursquare, Formspring, HootSuite, and Reddit, among others.[16] In addition, the failure propagated across multiple "availability zones." It was also reported that Amazon permanently lost some customer data.

Litigation and enforcement actions arising from security breaches of personal information are becoming common.[17] Lawsuits seeking class action status are proceeding against retailers, credit card issuers, payment processors, and banks. The Federal Trade Commission (FTC) has brought enforcement actions,[18] along with states' attorneys general, for violations of consumer protection laws amounting to unfair practices. Consumers have sued complaining that merchants, banks, and payment processors were negligent in their failure to protect their personal information.

STATE SECURITY BREACH NOTIFICATION LAWS

The imposition of data security and security breach notification obligations on entities that own, possess, or license personal information is a recent phenomenon. California was the first jurisdiction to enact a data breach notification law in 2002, requiring notification when unencrypted personal information was, or is reasonably believed to have been, acquired by an unauthorized person.[19] There followed the emergence of numerous federal and state bills modeled after the California law imposing notification requirements on entities that own, license, or process personal information. Many states, however, included an element of harm as a trigger for notification rather than simply unauthorized acquisition. For example, under Alaska law "disclosure is not required if, after an appropriate investigation and after written notification to the attorney general of this state, the covered person determines that there is not a reasonable likelihood that harm to the consumers whose personal information has been acquired has resulted or will result from the breach."[20]

The majority of states have enacted laws requiring notice of security breaches of personal data.[21] As of January 2012, 46 states, the District of Columbia, Puerto Rico, and the Virgin Islands have enacted laws requiring notification of security breaches involving personal information.[22] According to the National Conference of State Legislatures, in 2011 at least 14 states introduced legislation expanding the scope of laws, setting additional requirements related to notification, or changing penalties for those responsible for breaches. Several states have reportedly considered legislation to hold retailers liable for third-party companies' costs arising from data breaches.[23]

The Massachusetts security breach and data destruction law and security regulations[24] are considered to "constitute one of the most comprehensive sets of general security regulations yet seen at the state level.... [And] are clearly modeled after aspects of developing data security law at the federal level."[25] Alabama, Kentucky, New Mexico, and South Dakota do not have security breach notification laws. In September 2012, when the amended Texas breach notification law goes into effect, breach notification obligations will exist in all states because Texas will then require entities doing business within the state to provide notification of data breaches to residents of states that have not enacted their own breach notification law.[26] Thus, breach notification obligations will exist in all states because Texas's consumer notification obligations will apply not only to residents of Texas, but also to residents of states that don't have security breach notice requirements.[27]

Variations in state security breach notification law have been described as "so numerous that it is virtually impossible to convert these state laws into the more manageable format of fifty-state surveys."[28] Because states have different requirements, businesses engaged in interstate commerce are confronted with compliance challenges and cite the lack of uniformity as justification for a national security breach notification standard. State security breach notification laws have been criticized for creating "a fragmented, incoherent liability scheme."[29]

> The nature of any causal connection between security breaches and concrete harms suffered by consumers such as identity theft remains unclear. Because American consumers are not protected by a general right of information privacy, mere notice that a security breach has occurred is not associated with any right to compensation. Attempts to establish a right to damages following receipt of a security breach notice through class action lawsuits have generally only succeeded in clarifying the degree to which no such right exists, although many businesses suffering breaches have chosen on a voluntary basis to provide their customers with credit monitoring services to reduce the risk of harm from identity theft.[30]

Proponents of state security breach notification laws believe that state laboratories can provide stronger protection for sensitive personal information.[31]

Elements of Security Breach Notification Laws

State security breach notification laws generally follow a similar framework and can be categorized into several standard elements: (1) delineating who must comply with the law; (2) defining the terms "personal information" and "breach of security"; (3) establishing the elements of harm that must occur, if any, for notice to be triggered; (4) adopting requirements for notice; (5) creating exemptions and safe harbors; (6) clarifying preemption and relationships to other federal laws; and (7) creating penalties, enforcement authorities, and remedies.

State security breach notification laws vary regarding who is subject to the law—covered entities include businesses, state agencies, for profits, non-profits, information brokers, or persons conducting business within the state that own, license, or maintain the personal information of state residents. Twenty-nine states impose similar duties for the public and private sectors, 14 states do not, and Oklahoma's law applies only to the public sector.[32] State security breach notification laws generally apply to electronic or computerized data.

Security breach notification laws typically include definitions for "personal information" or "personally identifiable information." In information privacy law, there is no uniform definition of "personally identifiable information."[33] A common definition includes an individual's first name or initial and last name combined with SSN; driver's license or state ID number; account number, credit or debit card number, combined with any required information that allows access to account or any other financial information. A few states include medical information and/or health insurance information. Many states exclude from the definition of personal information any publicly available information that is lawfully made available to the general public from federal, state, or local government records. The term "sensitive personally identifiable information" is a subset of personally identifiable information (PII), the meaning of which also varies, but typically includes any information about an individual (including education, financial transactions, medical history, and criminal or employment history) along with information that can be used to distinguish or trace the individual's identity (including name, address, or telephone number; date and place of birth; mother's maiden name; Social Security number or other government-issued unique identification number; biometric data; or unique account identifiers).

The standard definition for "breach of security" is unauthorized acquisition of personal information that compromises the security, confidentiality, or integrity of personal information maintained by a covered entity.

In some states, the standard trigger for notice is the unauthorized access and acquisition of personal information. Some states require a risk of harm assessment to determine the level of harm or the risk of misuse involved. The results of the risk assessment determine whether notice is required.

State security breach notification laws describe who must provide notice (some require third-party service providers to notify the owner or licensor of the data when a breach occurs); recipients of notification (individuals, consumer reporting agencies for large scale breaches, state attorneys general); timing (following discovery or following unauthorized access, promptly, without unreasonable delay); methods (written, mail, email, substitute, mass media); content of notice; and delayed notification for law enforcement or national security purposes.

Many states provide a safe harbor for entities that are regulated under the Gramm-Leach-Bliley Act (GLBA) or the Health Insurance Portability and Accountability Act (HIPAA) and accompanying regulations and guidance. The safe harbor is generally available to entities that are in compliance with those laws, rules, regulations, or guidelines.

Forty-six states, the District of Columbia, Puerto Rico, and the Virgin Islands exempt encrypted information from notification requirements.[34]

Thirteen states, the District of Columbia, and Puerto Rico permit an individual to bring a private right of action to recover damages and/or obtain equitable relief from businesses for injuries from the breach, for failure to notify customers of a security breach in a timely manner, or under state consumer protection statutes (e.g., unfair or deceptive practices).[35] In some cases, prevailing plaintiffs are permitted to recover reasonable attorneys fees and court costs. Some permit the state attorney general to bring an action; other states only allow attorney general enforcement.[36]

Penalties may be included for failure to promptly notify customers of a security breach. Penalties vary from imposition of a civil penalty of up to $500, but not to exceed $50,000 for each state resident who was not notified; a civil penalty not to exceed $10,000 per breach; assessment of appropriate penalties and damages; $1,000 per day per breach, then up to $50,000 for each 30-day period up to 180 days not to exceed $500,000; $2,500 per violation and for any actual damages; state attorney general actions under state consumer protection laws which permit the imposition of significant fines, injunctive relief, and attorneys' fees; and identity theft penalties.

FEDERAL INFORMATION SECURITY AND SECURITY BREACH NOTIFICATION LAWS

The legal and regulatory framework for the protection of personally identifiable information is complex because businesses, governments, and individuals who process data must comply with the requirements of many differing privacy, information security, and breach notification laws. No single federal law or regulation governs the security of all types of sensitive personal information. Determining which federal law, regulation, and self-regulatory guidance is applicable depends in part on the entity or sector that collected the information, and the type of information collected and regulated.[37] Under federal law, certain sectors are legally obligated to protect certain types of sensitive personal information. These obligations were created, in large part, when federal privacy and security legislation was enacted in the credit, financial services, health care, government, securities, and Internet sectors. Federal regulations were issued to implement information security programs and provide standards for security breach notice to affected persons.[38]

For example, there are federal information security requirements applicable to all federal government agencies via the Federal Information Security Management Act (FISMA)[39] and a federal information security and security breach notification law applicable to a sole federal department (Veterans Affairs).[40] Federal departments and agencies are obligated by memorandum to provide breach notification, while the Department of Veterans Affairs is statutorily obligated to do so.

Other federal laws and regulations, such as the Health Insurance Portability and Accountability Act (HIPAA) and the Gramm-Leach-Bliley Act (GLBA), require private sector entities to maintain security safeguards to ensure the confidentiality, integrity, and availability of personal information, and require notification of security breaches.[41] In the private sector, different laws apply to private sector entities engaged in different businesses (such as HIPAA, the Health Information Portability and Accountability Act, and GLBA, Gramm-Leach-Bliley Act, discussed hereinafter). This is what is commonly referred to as a sectoral approach to the protection of personal information. The Federal Trade Commission Act (the FTC Act) prohibits unfair and deceptive practices in and affecting commerce.[42] The Payment Card Industry Data Security Standards (PCI-DSS) include information security requirements for organizations that handle bank cards.[43]

Some critics say that current laws focus too closely on industry-specific uses of information rather than on protecting the privacy of individuals.[44] Others believe the sectoral approach to the protection of personal information reflects not only variations in the types of information collected (e.g., government, private sector, health, financial, etc.), but also differences in the regulatory framework for particular sectors. Others advocate a national standard for entities that maintain personal information in order to harmonize legal obligations.[45] Others distinguish between private data held by the government and private data held by others, and advocate a higher duty of care for governments with respect to sensitive personal information in the U.S. public sector and to data breaches.[46]

This section describes information security and data breach notification requirements included in the Gramm-Leach-Bliley Act, the Health Insurance Portability and Accountability Act, and the Health Information Technology for

Economic and Clinical Health Act. Also discussed are implementing regulations, to the extent that they include data security and breach notification requirements, such as the FTC Safeguards Rule and the Information Security Interagency Guidance issued by the federal banking regulators. Because some of the federal security breach notification bills would also apply to federal agencies, we are including an overview of the Office of Management and Budget's "Breach Notification Policy" for federal agencies.

Office of Management and Budget "Breach Notification Policy" For Federal Agencies

In response to recommendations from the President's Identity Theft Task Force,[47] the Office of Management and Budget issued guidance in May 2007 for federal agencies on "Safeguarding Against and Responding to the Breach of Personally Identifiable Information."[48]

The OMB Memorandum M-07-16 requires all federal agencies to implement a breach notification policy to safeguard "personally identifiable information" by August 22, 2007, to apply to both electronic systems and paper documents.[49] To formulate their policy, agencies are directed to review existing privacy and security requirements, and include requirements for incident reporting and handling and external breach notification. In addition, agencies are required to develop policies concerning the responsibilities of individuals authorized to access personally identifiable information.

Attachment 1 of the OMB memorandum, *Safeguarding Against the Breach of Personally Identifiable Information*, reemphasizes agencies' responsibilities under existing law (e.g., the Privacy Act and FISMA), executive orders, regulations, and policy to safeguard personally identifiable information and train employees. New privacy and security requirements are established.

Agencies are required to review holdings of all personally identifiable information to ensure that they are accurate, relevant, timely, and complete, and reduced to the minimum necessary amount. Agencies must also establish a plan to eliminate the unnecessary collection and use of Social Security numbers.

Agencies must implement the following security requirements (applicable to all federal information): encrypt all data on mobile computers/devices carrying agency data; employ two-factor authentication for remote access; use a "time-out" function for remote access and mobile devices; log and verify all computer-readable data extracts from databases holding sensitive information; and ensure that individuals and supervisors with authorized access to personally identifiable information annually sign a document describing their responsibilities.[50]

Attachment 2 of the OMB Memorandum, *Incident Reporting and Handling Requirements*, applies to the breach of personally identifiable information in electronic or paper format.

Agencies are required to report all incidents involving personally identifiable information within one hour of discovery/detection, and publish a "routine use"[51] under the Privacy Act applying to the disclosure of information to appropriate persons in the event of a data breach.[52]

Attachment 3, *External Breach Notification*, identifies the factors agencies should consider in determining when notification outside the agency should be given and the nature of the notification. Notification may not be necessary for encrypted information.

Each agency is directed to establish an agency response team. Agencies must assess the likely risk of harm caused by the breach and the level of risk. Agencies should provide notification without unreasonable delay following the detection of a breach, but are permitted to delay notification for law enforcement, national security purposes, or agency needs. Attachment 3 also includes specifics as to the content of the notice, criteria for determining the method of notification, and the types of notice that may be used.

Attachment 4, *Rules and Consequences Policy*, directs each agency to develop and implement a policy outlining rules of behavior and identifying consequences and corrective actions available for failure to follow these rules. Supervisors may be subject to disciplinary action for failure to take appropriate action upon discovering the breach or failure to take required steps to prevent a breach from occurring.

Rules of behavior and corrective actions should address the failure to implement and maintain security controls for personally identifiable information; exceeding authorized access to, or disclosure to unauthorized persons of, personally identifiable information; failure to report any known or suspected loss of control or unauthorized disclosure of personally identifiable information; and for managers, failure to adequately instruct, train, or supervise employees in their responsibilities.

Consequences may include reprimand, suspension, removal, or other actions in accordance with applicable law and agency policy.

Health Insurance Portability and Accountability Act

Part C of the Health Insurance Portability and Accountability Act of 1996 (HIPAA)[53] requires "the development of a health information system through the establishment of standards and requirements for the electronic transmission of health information."[54] These "Administrative Simplification" provisions require the Secretary of Health and Human Services to adopt national standards to facilitate the electronic exchange of information; establish code sets for data elements; protect the privacy of individually identifiable health information; maintain administrative, technical, and physical safeguards for the security of health information; provide unique health identifiers; and to adopt procedures for the use of electronic signatures.[55]

HIPAA covered entities—health plans, health care clearinghouses, and health care providers who transmit financial and administrative transactions electronically—are required to comply with the national standards and regulations.[56] Under HIPAA, the Secretary is required to impose a civil monetary penalty on any person failing to comply with the national standards and regulations.[57] The minimum civil money penalty (i.e., the fine) for a violation is $100 per violation and up to $25,000 for all violations of an identical requirement or prohibition during a calendar year.[58] The maximum civil money penalty (i.e., the fine) for a violation is $50,000 per violation and up to $1,500,000 for all violations of an identical requirement or prohibition during a calendar year.[59] HIPAA also establishes criminal penalties for any person who knowingly and in violation of the Administrative Simplification provisions of HIPAA uses a unique health identifier, or obtains or discloses individually identifiable health information.[60] Enhanced criminal penalties may be imposed if the offense is committed under false pretenses, with intent to sell the information or reap other personal gain. The penalties include a fine of not more than $50,000 and/or imprisonment of not more than one year; if the offense is under false pretenses, a fine of not more than $100,000 and/or imprisonment of not more than five years; and if the offense is with intent to sell, transfer, or use individually identifiable health information for commercial advantage, personal gain, or malicious harm, a fine of not more than $250,000 and/or imprisonment of not more than 10 years.[61] These penalties do not affect other penalties imposed by other federal programs.

HIPAA Privacy Rule

HIPAA required adoption of a national privacy standard for the protection of individually identifiable health information.[62] HHS issued final Standards for Privacy of Individually Identifiable Health Information, known as the Privacy Rule, on April 14, 2003.[63] The HIPAA Privacy Rule is applicable to health plans, health care clearinghouses, and health care providers who transmit financial and administrative transactions electronically. The rule regulates "protected health information"[64] that is "individually identifiable health information"[65] transmitted by or maintained in electronic, paper, or any other medium. The Privacy Rule requires covered entities to enter into agreements with business associates who create, receive, maintain, or transmit protected health information (PHI) on their behalf. The Office of Civil Rights (OCR) in HHS enforces the Privacy Rule.[66]

The HIPAA Privacy Rule limits the circumstances under which an individual's protected health information may be used or disclosed by covered entities. A covered entity is permitted to use or disclose protected health information without patient authorization for treatment, payment, or health care operations.[67] For other purposes, a covered entity may only use or disclose PHI with patient authorization subject to certain exceptions.[68] Exceptions permit the use or disclosure of PHI without patient authorization or prior agreement for public health, judicial, law enforcement, and other specialized purposes.[69] In certain situations that would otherwise require authorization, a covered entity may use or disclose PHI without authorization provided that the individual is given the prior opportunity to object or agree.[70] The HIPAA Privacy Rule also requires a covered entity to maintain reasonable and appropriate administrative, technical, and physical safeguards to protect the privacy of protected health information.[71]

HIPAA Security Rule

HIPAA also required adoption of a national security standard for the protection of individually identifiable health information.[72] HHS issued the HIPAA Security Rule in 2003. The Security Rule applies only to protected health information in electronic form (EPHI), and requires a covered entity to ensure the confidentiality, integrity, and availability of all EPHI the covered entity creates, receives, maintains, or transmits.[73] Covered entities must protect against any reasonably anticipated threats or hazards to the security or integrity of such information and any reasonably anticipated uses or disclosures of such information that are not permitted or required under the Privacy Rule and ensure compliance by their workforces.[74] The Security Rule requires covered entities to enter into agreements with business associates who create, receive, maintain, or transmit EPHI on their behalf.[75] A covered entity is not liable for violations by the business associate unless the covered entity knew that the business associate was engaged in a practice or pattern of activity that violated HIPAA, and the covered entity failed to take corrective action. The Centers for Medicare and Medicaid Services (CMS) has been delegated authority to enforce the HIPAA Security Rule.[76]

The Security Rule allows covered entities to consider such factors as the cost of a particular security measure, the size of the covered entity involved, the complexity of the approach, the technical infrastructure and other security capabilities in place, and the nature and scope of potential security risks. The Security Rule establishes "standards" that covered entities must meet, accompanied by implementation specifications for each standard. The Security Rule identifies three categories of standards: administrative, physical, and technical.

Health Information Technology for Economic and Clinical Health Act (HITECH Act)

The Health Information Technology for Economic and Clinical Health Act (HITECH Act) was enacted as part of the American Recovery and Reinvestment Act of 2009 (ARRA).[77] As part of this new law, sweeping changes to the health information privacy regime were enacted. Most of the privacy provisions are additional requirements supplementing the HIPAA Privacy and Security Rules, but a few provisions deal specifically with electronic health records (EHRs).[78] The HITECH Act extended application of some provisions of the HIPAA Privacy and Security Rules to the business associates of HIPAA-covered entities, making those business associates subject to civil and criminal liability; established new limits on the use of protected health information for marketing and fundraising purposes; provided new enforcement authority for state attorneys general to bring suit in federal district court to enforce HIPAA violations; increased civil and criminal penalties for HIPAA violations; required covered entities and business associates to notify the public and HHS of data breaches; changed certain use and disclosure rules for protected health information; and created additional individual rights.

Business Associates' Civil and Criminal Liability

The HITECH Act provides that covered entities' business associates that obtain or create PHI pursuant to a business associate agreement may only use or disclose that PHI in compliance with its terms.[79] The HITECH Act also requires existing business associate agreements to incorporate the new privacy provisions.[80]

Prior to the HITECH Act, covered entities have been liable for violations of the Privacy Rule that were committed by their business associates, but only if the covered entity had knowledge of "a pattern of activity or practice" of the business associate that violates the Privacy Rule.[81] Under the HITECH Act, business associates are also made liable for violations of the Privacy Rule committed by the covered entities with which they contract, if the business associates are aware of a pattern and practice of unlawful conduct by the covered entity.[82] While business associates are still not defined as covered entities under HIPAA, they are subject to the same civil and criminal penalties for improper uses or disclosures of PHI.[83]

The HITECH Act also extended application of the HIPAA Security Rule's provisions on security safeguards and documentation to business associates of covered entities, making those business associates subject to civil and criminal liability for violations of the HIPAA Security Rule.[84] Under the HIPAA Security Rule, only covered entities can be held civilly or criminally liable for violations. While business associates are still not considered covered entities under HIPAA, they are subject to the same civil and criminal penalties as a covered entity for Security Rule violations.[85] The HITECH Act also requires existing business associate agreements to incorporate the new security requirements.[86]

Unsecured Protected Health Information

The HITECH Act required the HHS Secretary to issue guidance specifying the technologies and methodologies to render protected health information unusable, unreadable, or indecipherable to unauthorized individuals.[87] The HITECH Act also provides a definition.[88]

Guidance on the meaning of "unsecured protected health information" was issued by HHS that became effective upon issuance. It identified two methods for rendering PHI unusable, unreadable, or indecipherable: encryption and destruction (paper and electronic form). Pursuant to this guidance, "if PHI is rendered unusable, unreadable, or indecipherable to unauthorized individuals by one or more of the methods identified in this guidance, then such information is not 'unsecured' PHI." Because the HITECH Act's breach notification requirements apply only to breaches of unsecured PHI, this guidance provides the means by which covered entities and their business associates can determine whether a breach has occurred and whether notification obligations apply.[89]

Breach Notification

The Health Information Technology for Economic and Clinical Health Act (HITECH Act) imposed breach notification requirements on covered entities, their business associates, and vendors of personal health records (PHRs).[90] The HITECH Act requires covered entities, business associates, and vendors of PHRs to notify affected individuals in the event of a "breach" of "unsecured protected health information."[91] A "breach" is defined as the "unauthorized acquisition, access, use, or disclosure of protected health information which compromises the security or privacy of such information, except where an unauthorized person to whom such information is disclosed would not reasonably have been able to retain such information."[92] A vendor of PHR is defined as "an entity, other than a covered entity ... that offers or maintains a personal health record."[93] The term "unsecured protected health information" means "protected health information that is not secured through the use of a technology or methodology specified by the Secretary in guidance."[94]

In August 2009, the Department of Health and Human Services (HHS) issued an interim final breach notification regulation.[95] The Breach Notification Interim Final Regulation addresses notification to individuals, the media, and the Secretary, by a business associate; law enforcement delay; and administrative requirements and burdens of proof.

The HITECH Act also directed the Federal Trade Commission (FTC) to issue breach notification regulations for web-based businesses to notify consumers when the security of their electronic health information is breached.[96] The FTC rule applies to both vendors of personal health records—which provide online repositories that people can use to keep track of their health information—and entities that offer third-party applications for personal health records. It applies to breaches by vendors of PHRs, PHR-related entities, and third-party service providers that maintain information on U.S. citizens or residents.[97] The rule contains provisions discussing timeliness, methods of notification, content, and enforcement of the breach notification requirements.

Notice of Unauthorized Disclosure of Protected Health Information

The HITECH Act requires a covered entity to notify affected individuals when it discovers that their unsecured PHI has been, or is reasonably believed to have been, breached.[98] This requirement applies to covered entities that access, maintain, retain, modify, record, store, destroy, or otherwise hold, use, or disclose unsecured protected health information. The scope of notification is dependant upon the number of individuals whose unsecured PHI was compromised. Generally, only written notice need be provided if less than 500 individuals are involved. For larger breaches, notice through prominent media outlets may be required. In all cases, the Secretary of HHS must be notified, although breaches involving less than 500 people may be reported on an annual basis. The Secretary of HHS is directed to display on the department's website a list of covered entities with breaches involving more than 500 individuals.[99]

Generally, notice must be given without unreasonable delay, but no later than 60 days after the breach is discovered. If a delay is not reasonable, a covered entity may still have violated this provision even if notice was given within 60 days. In an enforcement action of this provision, the covered entity has the burden of proving that any delay was reasonable. Delayed notification is permitted for law enforcement purposes if a law enforcement official determines that notice would impede a criminal investigation or cause damage to national security.

To the extent possible, notification of a breach must include a description of what occurred; the types of information involved in the breach; steps individuals should take in response to the breach; what the covered entity is doing to investigate, mitigate, and protect against further harm; and contact information to obtain additional information.

Annually, the Secretary is required to submit a report to Congress containing information on the number and nature of breaches for which notice was provided and actions taken in response to such breaches.[100]

Notice of Unauthorized Disclosure of Personal Health Records

The HITECH Act includes a breach notification requirement for PHR vendors (such as Google Health or Microsoft Vault), service providers to PHR vendors, and PHR servicers that are not covered entities or business associates that sunsets "if Congress enacts new legislation."[101] Under this breach notification requirement, these entities are required to notify citizens and residents of the United States whose unsecured "PHR identifiable health information" has been, or is believed to have been, breached. PHR vendors, service providers to PHR vendors, and PHR servicers are also required to notify the Federal Trade Commission (FTC).[102]

The HITECH Act defines several terms specific to the PHR breach notification requirement. A "breach of security" is defined as the unauthorized acquisition of an individual's PHR identifiable health information.[103] PHR identifiable health information is defined as individually identifiable health information, and includes information provided by or on behalf of the individual, and information that can reasonably be used to identify the individual.[104]

The requirements regarding the scope, timing, and content of these notifications are identical to the requirements applicable to breaches of unsecured PHI. Violations of these requirements shall be considered unfair and deceptive trade practices in violation of the Federal Trade Commission Act.

Gramm-Leach-Bliley Act (GLBA)

Title V of the Gramm-Leach-Bliley Act of 1999 (GLBA) requires financial institutions to provide customers with notice of their privacy policies and requires financial institutions to safeguard the security and confidentiality of customer information, to protect against any anticipated threats or hazards to the security or integrity of such records, and to protect against unauthorized access to or use of such records or information which could result in substantial harm or inconvenience to any customer.[105] Financial institutions are defined as businesses that are engaged in certain "financial activities" described in Section 4(k) of the Bank Holding Company Act of 1956 and accompanying regulations.[106] Such activities include traditional banking, lending, and insurance functions, along with other financial activities. Financial institutions are prohibited from disclosing "nonpublic personal information"[107] to non-affiliated third parties without providing customers with a notice of privacy practices and an opportunity to opt out of the disclosure. A number of statutory exceptions are provided to this disclosure rule, including that financial institutions are permitted to disclose nonpublic personal information to a non-affiliated third party to perform services for or functions on behalf of the financial institution.

GLBA Privacy Rule

Regulations implementing GLBA's privacy requirements published by the federal banking regulators govern the treatment of nonpublic personal information about consumers by financial institutions;[108] require a financial institution in specified circumstances to provide notice to customers about its privacy policies and practices; describe the conditions under which a financial institution may disclose nonpublic personal information about consumers to nonaffiliated third parties; and provide a method for consumers to prevent a financial institution from disclosing that information to most nonaffiliated third parties by "opting out" of that disclosure, subject to exceptions.[109]

FTC Safeguards Rule

This rule implements GLBA's requirements for entities under FTC jurisdiction. The Safeguards Rule applies to all businesses, regardless of size, that are "significantly engaged" in providing financial products or services. These include, for example, check-cashing businesses, payday lenders, mortgage brokers, nonbank lenders, real estate appraisers, and professional tax preparers. The Safeguards Rule also applies to companies like credit reporting agencies and ATM operators that receive information about the customers of other financial institutions. The rule requires financial institutions to have an information security plan that "contains administrative, technical, and physical safeguards" to "insure the security and confidentiality of customer information: protect against any anticipated threats or hazards to the security or integrity of such information; and protect against unauthorized access to or use of such information that could result in substantial harm or inconvenience to any customer."[110] Using its authority under the Safeguards Rule, the commission has brought a number of enforcement actions to address the failure to provide reasonable and appropriate security to protect consumer information.[111]

GLBA Information Security Guidelines

Section 501(b) of GLBA requires the banking agencies to establish standards for financial institutions relating to administrative, technical, and physical safeguards to ensure the security, confidentiality, and integrity of customer information; protect against any anticipated threats or hazards to the security or integrity of such information; and protect against unauthorized access to or use of such information that could result in substantial harm or inconvenience to any customer.

Interagency Guidance issued by the federal banking regulators[112] applies to customer information, which is defined as "any record containing nonpublic personal information ... about a customer, whether in paper, electronic, or other form, that is maintained by or on behalf of" a financial institution.[113] The security guidelines direct each financial institution to assess the risks of reasonably foreseeable threats that could result in unauthorized disclosure, misuse, alteration, or destruction of customer information and customer information systems; the likelihood and potential damage of threats; and the sufficiency of policies, procedures, customer information systems, and other controls. Following the assessment of risks, the security guidelines require a financial institution to manage and control the risk through the design of a program to address the identified risks; train staff to implement the program; regularly test the key controls, systems, and procedures of the information security program; and develop and maintain appropriate measures to dispose of customer information. The security guidelines also direct every financial institution to require its service providers by contract to implement appropriate measures designed to protect against unauthorized access to or use of customer information that could result in substantial harm or inconvenience to any customer. Each financial institution is required to monitor, evaluate, and adjust its information security program as necessary. Finally, each financial institution is required to report to its board at least annually on its information security program, compliance with the security guidelines, and issues such as risk assessment, risk management and control decisions, service provider arrangements, results of testing, security breaches or violations and management's responses, and recommendations for changes in the information security program.

Response Programs for Unauthorized Access to Customer Information and Customer Notice

The security guidelines recommend implementation of a risk-based response program, including customer notification procedures, to address unauthorized access to or use of customer information maintained by a financial institution or its service provider that could result in substantial harm or inconvenience to any customer, and require disclosure of a data security breach if the covered entity concludes that "misuse of its information about a customer has occurred or is reasonably possible."[114] Pursuant to the guidance, substantial harm or inconvenience is most likely to result from improper access to "sensitive customer information."[115]

At a minimum, an institution's response program should contain procedures for assessing the nature and scope of an incident and identifying what customer information systems and types of customer information have been accessed or misused; notifying its primary federal regulator when the institution becomes aware of an incident involving unauthorized access to or use of sensitive customer information; consistent with the Agency's Suspicious Activity Report ("SAR") regulations, notifying appropriate law enforcement authorities; taking appropriate steps to contain and control the incident to prevent further unauthorized access to or use of customer information (e.g., by monitoring, freezing, or closing affected accounts and preserving records and other evidence); and notifying customers when warranted.

The security guidelines note that financial institutions have an affirmative duty to protect their customers' information against unauthorized access or use, and that customer notification of a security breach involving the customer's's information is a key part of that duty. The guidelines prohibit institutions from forgoing or delaying customer notification because of embarrassment or inconvenience.

The guidelines provide that when a financial institution becomes aware of an incident of unauthorized access to sensitive customer information, the institution should conduct a reasonable investigation to promptly determine the likelihood that the information has been or will be misused. If the institution determines that misuse has occurred or is reasonably possible, it should notify the affected customer as soon as possible. Customer notice may be delayed if an appropriate law enforcement agency determines that notification will interfere with a criminal investigation and provides the institution with a written request for the delay. The institution should notify its customers as soon as notification will no longer interfere with the investigation.

If a financial institution can determine which customers' information has been improperly accessed, it may limit notification to those customers whose information it determines has been misused or is reasonably likely to be misused. In situations where the institution determines that a group of files has been accessed improperly, but is unable to identify which specific customers' information has been accessed, and the institution determines that misuse of the information is reasonably possible, it should notify all customers in the group. The guidelines also address what information should be included in the notice sent to the financial institution's customers.

End Notes

[1] The Privacy Rights Clearinghouse reports that as of September 11, 2011 over 2,676 data breaches were made public since 2005 involving 535 million records containing sensitive personal information. Privacy Rights Clearinghouse, Chronology of Data Breaches Security Breaches 2005 – Present, at http://www.privacyrights.org/data-breach.

[2] United States v. ChoicePoint, Inc., No. 1:06-CV-0198 (N.D. Ga. Feb. 15, 2006), http://www.ftc.gov/os/caselist/ choicepoint/stipfinaljudgement.pdf (stipulated order imposing $15 million judgment); United States v. ChoicePoint, Inc., No. 1:06-CV-0198-

JTC (N.D. Ga. Oct. 14, 2009), http://www.ftc.gov/os/caselist/choicepoint/ 100902choice pointstip.pdf (stipulated order imposing additional $275,000 civil penalty).

[3] U.S. Securities and Exchange Commission, *Form 10-K Annual Report: The TJX Cos., Inc.,* http://www.sec.gov/ Archives/edgar/data/109198/000095013507001906/b64407 tje10vk.htm.

[4] Ross Kerber, Hannaford Case Exposes Holes In Law, Some Say "Identity Theft" Criteria Called Too Narrow, at http://www.boston.com/business/articles/2008/03/30/ hannaford _case_exposes_holes_in_law_some_say/?page=full.

[5] Former Connecticut Attorney General Richard Blumenthal sued Health Net of Connecticut for failing to secure private patient medical records and financial information involving 446,000 Connecticut enrollees and 1.5 million consumers nationwide and promptly notify consumers exposed by the security breach. Connecticut Attorney General's Office, Press Release: Attorney General Announces Health Net Settlement Involving Massive Security Breach Compromising Private Medical and Financial Info, July 6, 2010 at http://www.ct.gov/ag/cwp/view.asp?A=2341&Q= 462754.

[6] Kevin Sack, "Patient Data Posted Online in Major Breach of Privacy, *The N.Y. Times,* Sep. 8, 2011, at http://www.nytimes.com/2011/09/09/us/09breach.html?pagewanted=all.

[7] State of New York Public Service Commission, PSC Investigates Consumer Data Breach At NYSEG, RG&E (Jan. 23, 2012); at http://www3.dps.ny.gov/pscweb/WebFileRoom. nsf/ArticlesByCategory/1986D5ECA1917A8A8525798E005F81DD/$File/ pr12007.pdf? OpenElement.

[8] Ponemon Institute, Five Countries: Cost of Data Breach, April 19, 2010, at http://www.ponemon.org/local/upload/fckjail/generalcontent/18/file/2010%20Global%20C ODB.pdf.

[9] Douglas McLeod, "A Surprising Reticence: Computer Network Risk Coverage Is Growing, But Not As Fast As One Would Expect Given The Recent Spate Of Corporate Data Breaches," CBS Interactive Business Network Resource Library (Oct. 15, 2011).

[10] According to the Federal Trade Commission (FTC), identity theft is the most common complaint from consumers in all 50 states. Between January and December 2010, the Consumer Sentinel Network (CSN), a database of consumer complaints, received more than 1.3 million consumer complaints. Identity theft tops the list accounting for 19% of the complaints. Federal Trade Commission, "Consumer Sentinel Network Data Book for January—December 2010," March 2011, at http://www.ftc.gov/sentinel/reports/sentinel-annual-reports/sentinel-cy2010.pdf. See also CRS Report R40599, *Identity Theft: Trends and Issues*, by Kristin M. Finklea.

[11] Cloud Computing is a form of computing that relies on Internet-based services and resources to provide computing services. Examples include web-based e-mail applications (Gmail) and business applications that are accessed online through a browser, instead of a local computer.

[12] "Cloud Computing's Growing Pains: Break-Ins And Breakdowns," *The Economist,* April 28, 2011, at http://www.economist.com/node/18620774/print.

[13] Elinor Mills, "Who Is Epsilon And Why Does It Have My Data?," *cnet News,* April 6, 2011, at http://news.cnet.com/ 8301-27080_3-20051038-245.html.

[14] Sony Computer Entertainment and Sony Network Entertainment, Sony Customer Notification US States (excluding Puerto Rico and Massachusetts), at http://us.playstation.com/news/ consumeralerts/#us.

[15] Amazon Elastic Compute Cloud (Amazon EC2) at http://aws.amazon.com/ec2/.

[16] Jonathan Eunice, The Cloud Backlash (Apr. 29, 2011) at http://news.cnet.com/8301-31114_3-20058674- 258.html#ixzz1LPsfKptq.

[17] Picanso, Kathryn E. , Protecting Information Security Under A Uniform Data Breach Notification Law, 75 Fordham L. Rev. 355 2006-2007. This Note examines state and federal responses to information security issues and suggests a framework for legislation. Part I discusses the problems posed by poor information security, describes current federal and state efforts to secure information networks and disclose any breaches, and comments on the relationship between state and federal laws. Part II considers potential judicial and statutory approaches to protecting data security at the federal and state level and examines state litigation and analyzes issues confronting plaintiffs who seek to recover damages under a negligence theory. Federal proposals for a uniform data security and breach law are also considered, along with their potential impact on current state models. Finally, Part III concludes with a recommendation for a regulatory framework that addresses the concerns for uniform data security regulations while maintaining the consumer protections guaranteed under state legislation.

[18] See A Preliminary FTC Staff Report on Protecting Consumer Privacy in an Era of Rapid Change: A Proposed Framework for Businesses and Policymakers (Dec. 1, 2010), available at http://www.ftc.gov/os/2010/12/ 101201privacyreport.pdf.

[19] The California Security Breach Notification Act requires a state agency, or any person or business that owns or licenses computerized data that include personal information, to disclose any breach of security of the data to any resident of the state whose unencrypted personal information was, or is reasonably believed to have been, acquired by an unauthorized person. Exemptions are provided for encrypted information, for criminal investigations by law enforcement, and for breaches that are either immaterial or not "reasonably likely to subject the customers to unauthorized disclosure of personal information." Cal. Civil Code §1798.29, 1798.80-1789.84.

[20] Alaska Stat. §45.48.010.

[21] Alaska Stat. §45.48.010 et seq.; Ariz. Rev. Stat. §44-7501; Ark. Code §4-110-101 et seq.; Cal. Civ. Code §§56.06, 1785.11.2, 1798.29, 1798.82; Colo. Rev. Stat. §6-1-716; Conn. Gen Stat. 36a-701(b); Del. Code tit. 6, §12B-101 et seq.; Fla. Stat. §817.5681; Ga. Code §§10-1-910, -911; Haw. Rev. Stat. §487N-2; Idaho Stat. §§28-51-104 to 28-51- 107; 815 ILCS 530/1 et seq.; Ind. Code §§24-4.9 et seq., 4-1-11 et seq.; Iowa Code §715C.1; Kan. Stat. 50-7a01, 50- 7a02; La. Rev. Stat. §51:3071 et seq.; Me. Rev. Stat. tit. 10 §§1347 et seq.; Md. Code, Com. Law §14-3501 et seq.; Mass. Gen. Laws §93H-1 et seq.; Mich. Comp. Laws §445.72; Minn. Stat. §§325E.61, 325E.64; Mississippi 2010 H.B. 583 (effective July 1, 2011); Mo. Rev. Stat. §407.1500; Mont. Code §§30-14-1704, 2-6-504; Neb. Rev. Stat. §§87-801, -802, -803, -804, -805, -806, -807; Nev. Rev. Stat. 603A.010 et seq.; N.H. Rev. Stat. §§359-C:19, -C:20, -C:21; N.J. Stat. 56:8-163; N.Y. Gen. Bus. Law §899-aa; N.C. Gen. Stat §75-65; N.D. Cent. Code §51-30-01 et seq.; Ohio Rev. Code §§1347.12, 1349.19, 1349.191, 1349.192; Okla. Stat. §74-3113.1 and §24-161 to -166; Oregon Rev. Stat. §646A.600 et seq.; 73 Pa. Stat. §2303; R.I. Gen. Laws §11-49.2-1 et seq.; S.C. Code §39-1-90; Tenn. Code §47-18- 2107, 2010 S.B. 2793; Tex. Bus. & Com. Code §521.03; Utah Code §§13-44-101, -102, -201, -202, -310; Vt. Stat. tit. 9 §2430 et seq.; Va. Code §18.2-186.6, §32.1-127.1:05 (effective January 1, 2011); Wash. Rev. Code §19.255.010, 42.56.590; W.V. Code §§46A-2A-101 et seq.; Wis. Stat. §134.98 et seq.; Wyo. Stat. §40-12-501 to -502; D.C. Code §28- 3851 et seq.; 10 Laws of Puerto Rico §4051 et. seq.; V.I. Code §2208. See State Security Breach Notification Laws, Nat'l Conference Of State

Legislatures,   http://www.ncsl.org/issues-research/telecommunications-information-technology/security-breach-notification-laws.aspx (last updated Oct. 12, 2010).

[22] The Commercial Law League of America, State Data Security / Breach Notification Laws (As of December 2011), at http://www.clla.org/. Click "Resources," Click "Data Breach Notification Laws By State."

[23] California, Connecticut, Illinois, Massachusetts, Minnesota, New Jersey, Texas, and Wisconsin.

[24] 201 CMR 17.00 *et seq.* The Massachusetts regulations require "all persons that own, license, store or maintain personal information about a resident of Massachusetts" to protect the security and confidentiality of personal information about residents and require companies to implement a comprehensive written information security program (based on listed requirements) and to deploy security safeguards (encryption). By March 1, organizations holding the personal information of Massachusetts residents (including customers, employees and others, regardless of which state the data is stored in) must amend their vendor contracts to require compliance. 201 CMR 17.03(f)(2

[25] Smedinghoff, Thomas J. , "New State Regulations Signal Significant Expansion Of Corporate Data Security Obligations," *BNA Privacy & Security Law Report*, October 20, 2008, at http://www.wildman.com/article/
New_State_Regulations_Signal_Significant_Expansion.pdf.

[26] Kristen J. Mathews, Proskauer Privacy Law Blog: Breach Notification Obligations In All 50 States?, at http://privacylaw.proskauer.com/2011/08/articles/security-breach-notification-l/breach-notification-obligations-in-all50-states/.

[27] Tex. Bus. & Com. Code 521.03.

[28] Tom, Jacqueline May, A Simple Compromise: The Need for a Federal Data Breach Notification Law, 84 St. John's L. Rev. 1569 (2010) The author argues that a strict federal data breach notification law would appease business and increase incentives to disclose by reducing compliance costs and compliance risks.

[29] Winn, Jane K., Are "Better" Security Breach Notification Laws Possible? 2-3 (June 8, 2009). Berkley Technology Law Journal, Vol. 24, 2009. Available at SSRN: http://ssrn.com/abstract=1416222.

[30] *Id.*

[31] U.S. Congress, House Committee on Energy and Commerce, Subcommittee on Commerce, Manufacturing, and Trade, *The Threat Of Data Theft To American Consumers*, Hearing, 112th Cong., 1st sess., May 4, 2011, S. Hrg. 112–44 (Washington: GPO, 2011), p. 60.

[32] Kristen J. Mathews, Proskauer Privacy Law Blog: Breach Notification Obligations In All 50 States?, at http://privacylaw.proskauer.com/2011/08/articles/security-breach-notification-l/breach-notification-obligations-in-all50-states/.

[33] Schwartz, Paul M. and Solove, Daniel J., The PII Problem: Privacy and a New Concept of Personally Identifiable Information (December 05, 2011). New York University Law Review, Vol. 86, p. 1814, 2011. Available at SSRN: http://ssrn.com/abstract=1909366. ("Personally identifiable information (PII) is one of the most central concepts in information privacy regulation. The scope of privacy laws typically turns on whether PII is involved. The basic assumption behind the applicable laws is that if PII is not involved, then there can be no privacy harm. At the same time, there is no uniform definition of PII in information privacy law. Moreover, computer science has shown that in many circumstances non-PII can be linked to individuals, and that de-identified data can be re-identified.")

[34] See Burdon, M, Low, R and Reid, J, "If its Encrypted its Secure! The Viability of US State-based Encryption Exemptions" (Paper presented at the IEEE International Symposium on

Technology and Society, University of Wollongong, 7-9 June 2010). Available at SSRN: http://ssrn.com/abstract=1697930 ("Safe harbours to notification exist if personal information is encrypted....The underlying assumption of exemptions is that encrypted personal information is secure and therefore unauthorized access does not pose a risk. However, the viability of this assumption is questionable when examined against data breaches involving encrypted information and the demanding practical requirements of effective encryption management.")

[35] Alaska, California, Louisiana, Maryland, Massachusetts, Nevada, New Hampshire, North Carolina, Oregon, South Carolina, Tennessee, Virginia, Washington, District of Columbia, and Puerto Rico.

[36] The Commercial Law League of America, State Data Security / Breach Notification Laws (As of December 2011), at http://www.clla.org/. Click "Resources," Click "Data Breach Notification Laws By State."

[37] See CRS Report RL34120, *Federal Information Security and Data Breach Notification Laws*, by Gina Stevens.

[38] Smedinghoff, Thomas J. , The State of Information Security Law: A Focus on the Key Legal Trends (May 2008). Available at SSRN: http://ssrn.com/abstract=1114246 or http://dx.doi.org/10.2139/ssrn.1114246.

[39] Title III of the E-Government Act of 2002, P.L. 107-347; 44 U.S.C. §3541 *et seq.*

[40] The Veterans Benefits, Health Care, and Information Technology Act of 2006, P.L. 109-461; 38 U.S.C. §§5722 *et seq.* Title IX of P.L. 109-461, the Veterans Affairs Information Security Act, requires the Department of Veterans Affairs (VA) to implement agency-wide information security procedures to protect the VA's "sensitive personal information" (SPI) and VA information systems. In the event of a "data breach" of sensitive personal information processed or maintained by the VA Secretary, the Secretary must ensure that, as soon as possible after discovery, either a non-VA entity or the VA's Inspector General conduct an independent risk analysis of the data breach to determine the level of risk associated with the data breach for the potential misuse of any sensitive personal information. Based upon the risk analysis, if the Secretary determines that a reasonable risk exists of the potential misuse of sensitive personal information, the Secretary must provide credit protection services.

[41] Subpart D—Notification in the Case of Breach of Unsecured Protected Health Information, 45 C.F.R. Part 164.400 *et seq.* (upon discovery that unsecured protected health information has been, or is reasonably believed to have been breached); Health Breach Notification Rule, 16 C.F.R.§318 ((requiring entities to provide breach notification to an individual if they have a reasonable basis to believe the data can be linked to that individual); Office of Management and Budget Memorandum M-07-16, Memorandum on "Safeguarding Against and Responding to the Breach of Personally Identifiable Information," at http://www.whitehouse.gov/omb/memoranda/fy2007/m07-16.pdf (requires all federal agencies to implement a breach notification policy to safeguard "personally identifiable information" in electronic systems and paper documents); The Veterans Affairs Information Security Act, Title IX of P.L. 109-461, codified at 38 U.S.C. §23 *et seq.*, 38 C.F. R. Part 75, Information Security Matters ("With respect to individuals found under this subpart by the Secretary to be subject to a reasonable risk for the potential misuse of any sensitive personal information, the Secretary will promptly provide written notification by first-class mail to the individual (or the next of kin if the individual is deceased) at the last known address of the individual."); 12 C.F.R. Part 30, App. B.— Interagency Guidelines Establishing Information Security Standards ("When a financial institution becomes aware of an incident

of unauthorized access to sensitive customer information, the institution should conduct a reasonable investigation to promptly determine the likelihood that the information has been or will be misused. If the institution determines that misuse of its information about a customer has occurred or is reasonably possible, it should notify the affected customer as soon as possible.")

[42] 15 U.S.C. §§41-58. The Federal Trade Commission has used its Section 5 authority of the FTC Act in enforcing the Safeguard Rule of the Gramm-Leach-Bliley Act to determine whether a company's information security measures were reasonable and appropriate. The Safeguards Rule requires companies to develop a written information security plan to protect customer information.

[43] The Payment Card Industry Data Security Standards (PCI DSS) is an industry regulation developed by VISA, MasterCard, and other bank card distributors. It requires organizations that handle bank cards to conform to security standards and follow certain leveled requirements for testing and reporting. The core of the PCI DSS is a group of principles and accompanying requirements designed to build and maintain a secure network, protect cardholder data, maintain a vulnerability management program, implement strong access control measures, monitor and test networks, and maintain an information security policy. Available at https://www.pcisecuritystandards.org/security_standards/ pci_dss.shtml. Washington, Minnesota, and Nevada enacted laws incorporating all or part of the PCI DSS standard. Wash. H.B. 1149 (2010); Minn. Stat. §325E.64; Nev. Rev. Stat. Ch. 603A.

[44] Tom Zeller, Jr., *"Breach Points Up Flaws in Privacy Laws,"* N.Y. Times, Feb. 24, 2005 at A1.

[45] *Commercial Data Privacy and Innovation in the Internet Economy: A Dynamic Policy Framework* 7, available at http://www.commerce.gov/sites/default/files/ documents/2010/december/iptf-privacy-green-paper.pdf. ("Finally, we recommend the consideration of a Federal commercial data security breach notification (SBN) law that sets national standards, addresses how to reconcile inconsistent State laws, and authorizes enforcement by State authorities....This recommendation, however, is not meant to suggest preempting of other federal security breach notification laws, including those for specific sectors, such as healthcare.")

[46] A. Michael Froomkin, "Government Data Breaches," *University of Miami Legal Studies Research Paper No. 2009- 20.* Available at SSRN: http://ssrn.com/abstract=1427964.

[47] Exec. Order No. 13,402, 71 FR 27945 (2006); The President's Identity Theft Task Force, *Combating Identity Theft: A Strategic Plan*, April 2007 at http://www.identitytheft.gov/ reports/StrategicPlan.pdf.

[48] http://www.whitehouse.gov/omb/memoranda/fy2007/m07-16.pdf.

[49] The memo defines the term "personally identifiable information" as "information which can be used to distinguish or trace an individual's identity, such as their name, social security number, biometric records, etc. alone, or when combined with other personal or identifying information which is linked or linkable to a specific individual, such as date and place of birth, mother's maiden name, etc." *Id.*

[50] The first four information security requirements were adopted in an earlier memorandum, See OMB Memo 06-16, "Protection of Sensitive Agency Information" at http://www.white house.gov/omb/memoranda/fy2006/m06-16.pdf.

[51] The Privacy Act defines a routine use to mean "with respect to the disclosure of a record, the use of such record for a purpose which is compatible with the purpose for which it was collected." 5 U.S.C. §552a(a)(7).

[52] OMB Memorandum M-07-16, p.11.

[53] P.L. 104-191, 110 Stat. 1936 (1996), codified in part at 42 U.S.C. §§1320d *et seq.;* see CRS Report RL33989, *Enforcement of the HIPAA Privacy and Security Rules,* by Gina Stevens.

[54] 42 U.S.C. §§1320d—1320d-8.

[55] 42 U.S.C. §§1320d-2(a)-(d).

[56] 42 U.S.C. §1320d-4(b).

[57] 42 U.S.C. §1320d-5(a).

[58] 42 U.S.C. §1320d-5(a)(1). The HITECH Act, P.L. 111-5, increased civil and criminal penalties for some HIPAA violations. See CRS Report R40546, *The Privacy and Security Provisions for Health Information in the American Recovery and Reinvestment Act of 2009,* by Gina Stevens and Edward C. Liu.

[59] 42 U.S.C. §1320d-5(a)(1).

[60] 42 U.S.C. §1320d-6.

[61] 42 U.S.C. §1320d-6(b).

[62] "The term 'individually identifiable health information' means any information, including demographic information collected from an individual, that - (A) is created or received by a health care provider, health plan, employer, or health care clearinghouse; and (B) relates to the past, present, or future physical or mental health or condition of an individual, the provision of health care to an individual, or the past, present, or future payment for the provision of health care to an individual, and - (i) identifies the individual; or (ii) with respect to which there is a reasonable basis to believe that the information can be used to identify the individual." 42 U.S.C. §1320d(6).

[63] 45 C. F.R. Part 164 Subpart E—Privacy of Individually Identifiable Health Information.

[64] The definition of protected health information (PHI) excludes individually identifiable health information contained in certain education records and employment records held by a covered entity in its role as employer.

[65] 45 C.F.R. §160.103.

[66] 65 Fed. Reg. 82381.

[67] 45 C.F.R. §164.506.

[68] 45 C.F.R. §164.508.

[69] 45 C.F.R. §164.512(a)-(l).

[70] 45 C.F.R. §164.510.

[71] 45 C.F.R. §164.530(c).

[72] 42 U.S.C. §§1320d-2 and (d)(4).

[73] 45 C.F.R. §164.306(a).

[74] Dep't of Health and Human Services, Security 101 for Covered Entities at http://www.hhs.gov/ocr/privacy/hipaa/ administrative/securityrule/security101.pdf.

[75] Under such agreements, the business associate must: implement administrative, physical and technical safeguards that reasonably and appropriately protect the confidentiality, integrity and availability of the covered entity's electronic protected health information; ensure that its agents and subcontractors to whom it provides the information do the same; and report to the covered entity any security incident of which it becomes aware. The contract must also authorize termination if the covered entity determines that the business associate has violated a material term.

[76] HIPAA Security Standards for the Protection of Electronic Personal Health Information, 45 C.F.R. Part 164.302 – 164.318. See generally, Centers for Medicare and Medicaid Services, *Security Materials* at http://www.hhs.gov/ocr/ privacy/hipaa/administrative/securityrule/ securityruleguidance.html.

[77] P.L. 111-5.

[78] An electronic health record is defined as "an electronic record of health-related information on an individual that is created, gathered, managed, and consulted by authorized health care clinicians and staff." P.L. 111-5, §13400(5).

[79] P.L. 111-5, §13401(c).

[80] P.L. 111-5, §13404(a).

[81] 45 C.F.R. §164.504(e)(1)(ii).

[82] P.L. 111-5, §13404(b).

[83] P.L. 111-5, §§13401(b), 13404(c).

[84] P.L. 111-5, §13401. The HITECH Act adopts the same definition of business associates as the HIPAA Privacy and Security Rules. 45 C.F.R. §160.103.

[85] P.L. 111-5, §§13401(b), 13404(c).

[86] P.L. 111-5, §13404(a).

[87] P.L. 111-5, §13402(h).

[88] Under the default definition, PHI is unsecured if "it is not secured by a technology standard that renders protected health information unusable, unreadable, or indecipherable to unauthorized individuals and that is developed or endorsed by a standards developing organization that is accredited by the American National Standards Institute."

[89] *Id.* at 15-16.

[90] A personal health record (PHR) is defined as "an electronic record of identifiable health information on an individual that can be drawn from multiple sources and that is managed, shared, and controlled by or primarily for the individual." P.L. 111-5, §13400(11). A vendor of PHR is defined as "an entity, other than a covered entity ... that offers or maintains a personal health record." P.L. 111-5, §13400(18).

[91] P.L. 111-5, §§13402, 13407.

[92] P.L. 111-5, §13400(1). Not included in the definition of breach are any unintentional acquisition, use, or access of PHI by an employee or other authorized individual of a covered entity or a business associate done in good faith and within the scope of employment or the relationship where such information is not breached any further; or inadvertent disclosures by authorized persons of PHI within the same facility; and information received as a result of such disclosure is not further disclosed without authorization.

[93] P.L. 111-5, §13400(18).

[94] P.L. 111-5, §13402(h).

[95] P.L. 111-5, §13402(j); Subpart D—Notification in the Case of Breach of Unsecured Protected Health Information, 45 C.F.R. Part 164.400 *et seq.*

[96] Health Breach Notification Rule, 16 C.F.R. §318.

[97] *Id.*

[98] P.L. 111-5, §13402(a).

[99] http://www.hhs.gov/ocr/privacy/hipaa/administrative/breachnotificationrule/breachtool.html.

[100] P.L. 111-5, §13402(i).

[101] P.L. 111-5, §13407(g)(2). For further information on electronic personal health records, *see* CRS Report RS22760, *Electronic Personal Health Records*, by Gina Stevens.

[102] The FTC is directed to also notify the Secretary of HHS in the event of a breach.

[103] P.L. 111-5, §13407(f)(1).

[104] P.L. 111-5, §13407(f)(2).

[105] 15 U.S.C. §6801 - 6809. *See* CRS Report RS20185, *Privacy Protection for Customer Financial Information*, by M. Maureen Murphy.

[106] 12 U.S.C. §1843(k).

[107] (4) Nonpublic personal information.

(A) The term "nonpublic personal information" means personally identifiable financial information—

(i) provided by a consumer to a financial institution;

(ii) resulting from any transaction with the consumer or any service performed for the consumer; or

(iii) otherwise obtained by the financial institution.

(B) Such term does not include publicly available information, as such term is defined by the regulations prescribed under section 6804 of this title.

(C) Notwithstanding subparagraph (B), such term—

(i) shall include any list, description, or other grouping of consumers (and publicly available information pertaining to them) that is derived using any nonpublic personal information other than publicly available information; but

(ii) shall not include any list, description, or other grouping of consumers (and publicly available information pertaining to them) that is derived without using any nonpublic personal information. 15 U.S.C. §6809(4).

[108] 16 C.F.R. Part 13 (FTC); 12 C.F.R. Parts 40 (OCC), 216 (FRB), 332 (FDIC), 573 (OTS), and 716 (NCUA).

[109] See generally, 12 C.F.R. §225.28, §225.86.

[110] Standards for Insuring the Security, Confidentiality, Integrity and Protection of Customer Records and Information, 16 C.F.R. Part 314.

[111] For information on enforcement actions the Commission has brought involving the privacy of consumer information under Section 5 of the FTC Act, see http://www.ftc.gov/privacy/privacyinitiatives/safeguards_enf.html.

[112] See 12 C.F.R. Part 30, App. B (national banks); 12 C.F.R. Part 208, App. D-2 and Part 255, App. F (state member banks and holding companies); 12 C.F.R. Part 364, App. B (state non-member banks); 12 C.F.R. Part 570, App. B (savings associations); 12 C.F.R. Part 748, App. A (credit unions).

[113] See Board of Governors Federal Reserve System, The Commercial Bank Examination Manual, Supp. 27, 984-1034 (May 2007), at http://www.federalreserve.gov/boarddocs/SupManual/cbem/200705/0705cbem.pdf.

[114] Interagency Guidance on Response Programs for Unauthorized Access to Customer Information and Customer Notice, Part III of Supplement A to Appendix, at 12 C.F.R. Part 30 (OCC), Supplement A to Appendix D-2, at 12 C.F.R. Part 208 (Federal Reserve System), 12 C.F.R. Part 364 (FDIC), and 12 C.F.R. Part 568 (Office of Thrift Supervision), 70 Fed. Reg. 15736 - 15754 (March 29, 2005).

[115] "Sensitive customer information means a customer's name, address, or telephone number, in conjunction with the customer's social security number, driver's license number, account number, credit or debit card number, or a personal identification number or password that would permit access to the customer's account. Sensitive customer information also includes any combination of components of customer information that would allow someone to log onto or access the customer's account, such as user name and password or password and account number." 70 Fed. Reg. 15736-15754 (March 29, 2005).

In: Data Security Breaches   ISBN: 978-1-62257-735-4
Editors: P. Diaz and W. C. Long   © 2013 Nova Science Publishers, Inc.

Chapter 2

SELECTED FEDERAL DATA SECURITY BREACH LEGISLATION*

Kathleen Ann Ruane

SUMMARY

The protection of data, particularly data that can be used to identify individuals, has become an issue of great concern to Congress. There is no comprehensive federal law governing the protection of data held by private actors. Only those entities covered by the Gramm-Leach-Bliley Act, 15 U.S.C. §§6801-6809, (certain financial institutions) and the Health Insurance Portability and Accountability Act (HIPAA), 42 U.S.C. §1320d *et seq.*, and amendments to HIPAA contained in the Health Information Technology for Economic and Clinical Health Act (HITECH Act), P.L. 111-5, (certain health care facilities) are required explicitly by federal law to report data breaches. If private companies have indicated in their privacy policies that they will notify individuals upon a suspected data breach, failure to provide such notification may be considered to be an unfair and deceptive trade practice under Section 5 of the Federal Trade Commission Act (FTC Act). However, the FTC does not explicitly require private actors in possession of data related to individuals to notify individuals or the federal government should a data breach occur.

Forty-six states, the District of Columbia, Puerto Rico, and the Virgin Islands have enacted laws requiring notification upon a data

---

* This is an edited, reformatted and augmented version of Congressional Research Service, Publication No. R42474, dated April 9, 2012.

security breach involving personal information. However, these laws may vary in their application. They may only apply to certain entities or to certain data. Furthermore, companies maintaining stores of personal data may find it difficult to comply with the potentially different requirements of various state laws. A combination of a lack of a comprehensive federal law addressing security breaches involving personal data and the difficulty industry participants report in complying with various state laws has led Congress to propose a number of bills that would require private actors in possession of personal data to report breaches of that data. The Senate Judiciary Committee recently approved and reported three bills that would create federal standards for data breach notification: S. 1151, the Personal Data Privacy and Security Act of 2011 (Chairman Leahy); S. 1408, the Data Breach Notification Act of 2011 (Senator Feinstein); and S. 1535, the Personal Data Protection and Breach Accountability Act of 2011 (Senator Blumenthal). The bills have similar structures and elements. This chapter will analyze the bills, as reported out of the committee, discussing their similarities and differences.

INTRODUCTION

The protection of data, particularly data that can be used to identify individuals, has become an issue of great concern to Congress. There is no comprehensive federal law governing the protection of data held by private actors. Only those private entities covered by the GrammLeach-Bliley Act, 15 U.S.C. §§6801-6809, (certain financial institutions) and the Health Insurance Portability and Accountability Act (HIPAA), 42 U.S.C. §1320d et seq., and amendments to HIPAA contained in the Health Information Technology for Economic and Clinical Health Act (HITECH Act), P.L. 111-5, (certain health care facilities) are required explicitly by federal law to report data breaches. If private companies have indicated in their privacy policies that they will notify individuals upon a suspected data breach, failure to provide such notification may be considered to be an unfair and deceptive trade practice under Section 5 of the Federal Trade Commission Act (FTC Act). However, the FTC does not explicitly require private actors in possession of data related to individuals to notify individuals or the federal government should a data breach occur.

Forty-six states, the District of Columbia, Puerto Rico, and the Virgin Islands have enacted laws requiring notification upon a data security breach involving personal information.[1] However, these laws may vary in their application. They may only apply to certain entities or to certain data. Furthermore, companies maintaining stores of personal data may find it difficult to comply with the potentially different requirements of various state laws.[2] A combination of a lack of a comprehensive federal law addressing security breaches involving personal data and the difficulty industry participants report in complying with various state laws have led Congress to propose a number of bills that would require private actors and government agencies in possession of personal data to report breaches of that data. The Senate Judiciary Committee recently approved and reported three bills that would create federal standards for data breach notification: S. 1151, the Personal Data Privacy and Security Act of 2011 (Chairman Leahy); S. 1408, the Data Breach Notification Act of 2011 (Senator Feinstein); and S. 1535, the Personal Data Protection and Breach Accountability Act of 2011 (Senator Blumenthal). The bills have similar structures and elements. This chapter will analyze the bills, as reported out of the committee, discussing their similarities and differences. There have been other data security bills introduced in this Congress, as well, but they have yet to be reported out of their respective committees.[3] In the interest of brevity and clarity, they will not be discussed in this chapter.

SELECTED FEDERAL DATA SECURITY LEGISLATION

The three bills reported out the Senate Judiciary Committee have common elements and structure. All three bills would require notice of data security breaches, with certain exemptions. Each bill would attach penalties to a failure to provide notice in violation of the proposals. Each bill would preempt certain other state laws insofar as they would overlap with the new federal law. Two of the bills would require the creation and maintenance of data security programs. The bills have important differences as well. For example, S. 1151 contains amendments and additions to the crimes of identity theft and other criminal violations. S. 1535 would create a clearinghouse for technical information related to system vulnerabilities that would be maintained by a new government office. These, and other important differences, will be highlighted below.

Application

Before discussing the requirements of the proposed legislation, it is important to understand what entities the proposals would apply to and what types of information they would seek to protect. All three of the bills would apply to business entities (both for-profit and not-for-profit) and government agencies that collect and store sensitive, personally identifiable information. The bills also carve out certain exceptions for businesses to the extent that they are acting as "service providers." Each of the bills has slightly different definitions for each of these terms of art, but the spirit of their application remains substantially similar.

Entities Covered by the Bills

Agencies are defined as federal agencies by all three bills. Business entities cover all forms of business including corporations, partnerships, and other types of ventures. Service providers are defined as a business entity that provides electronic data transmission routing intermediate and transient storage or connections to its system or network where the business entity providing such services does not select or modify the content; is not the sender or intended recipient of the information; and the business entity transmits, routes, stores, or provides connections for personal information in a manner that personal information is undifferentiated from other types of data that such business entity transmits. Service providers are only treated as service providers to the extent that they are engaged in transmission services. If service providers hold or transmit data in such a way as to otherwise be covered by the proposals, then they would be required to comply with the proposals' requirements.

S. 1408 and S. 1535 also contain specific definitions for data brokers (or information brokers in the case of S. 1408). Both bills define these as commercial entities engaged in the business of collecting and assembling personal information of individuals who are not current or former customers of that entity for the purposes of selling that information to third parties. S. 1535 requires the entities to have information pertaining to at least 5,000 individuals who aren't customers or employees of that particular business entity to be covered by the definition of data broker, as well.

Data Covered by the Bills

All three bills would protect sensitive, personally identifiable information. They would define sensitive, personally identifiable information as the first and last name of an individual (or first initial and last name) plus some other piece of identifying information, such as a birth date, Social Security number, bank or credit card number, driver's license number, or other government indentifying number. S. 1408 seems to have the most restrictive definition of sensitive, personally identifiable information, because it would require an individual's first and last name (or first initial and last name) to be part of the information covered, plus another identifying piece of information. However, S. 1408 also grants the Federal Trade Commission (FTC) the authority to modify the types of information considered to be sensitive, personally identifiable information if such modification would not unreasonably impede interstate commerce, which may allow the agency to expand the types of data that would be covered by the bill.

S. 1151 and S. 1535 define sensitive, personally identifiable information more expansively, with S. 1535 having the most expansive definition of all three bills. Both S. 1151 and S. 1535 would define sensitive, personally identifiable information to include the information above as well as an individual's first and last name plus his or her home address, phone number, mother's maiden name, or birth date. The definition would also include a nontruncated Social Security number, driver's license number, passport number, alien registration number, or other government-issued unique identifier on its own; cellphone GPS location; fingerprints, voice prints, retina scans, or other "biometric data"; or other unique account identifiers, such as financial account numbers, credit card numbers, etc.

S. 1535 would also include in the definition of sensitive, personally identifiable information not less than two of the following: first and last name, unique account identifier, security code access code or password, and information regarding medical history. Most expansively, S. 1535 would include in the definition of sensitive, personally identifiable information any combination of data elements that could allow unauthorized access to or acquisition of the information described above.

Notice Requirement

Each of the bills would require business entities and agencies to notify individuals and the government, under certain circumstances, when there is a security breach involving sensitive, personally identifiable information, unless an exception or an exemption would apply. The bills would define security breach as the compromise of the security, confidentiality, or integrity of, or the loss of, computerized data that results in the unauthorized acquisition of, or unauthorized access to, sensitive, personally identifiable information.

Notice to Individuals Whose Information Was Subject to a Security Breach

The bills would require the notification of individuals whose sensitive, personally identifiable information was breached to occur in a timely fashion. If the business entity or agency is not the owner of the information that has been breached, the business or agency must notify the owner or licensee of the information of the breach. The business entity or agency will not be required to notify the individuals whose information has been breached if the owner or licensee provides the notification.

The notification requirement is also different for companies that are service providers. Service providers that become aware of a security breach that has occurred over their systems must notify the business entity or agency that originated the communication or transfer of sensitive, personally identifiable information that was breached. At which point, the business entity or agency that initiated the communication would then be required to comply with the notification requirements described above.

As noted, notification must occur in a timely fashion. Timeliness is defined as "without unreasonable delay." Businesses and agencies may take the time necessary, following a security breach, to determine the scope of the breach and take steps to prevent further or ongoing security breaches. They may also conduct risk assessments, discussed in more detail below, and take the time to restore the integrity of their data protection systems. A delay of longer than 60 days would be considered unreasonable, unless the FTC, or other agency with authority to do so, grants an extension, or an exception applies.

All of the bills allow notification to be delayed for law enforcement purposes. They also allow companies to avoid the notification requirement entirely if the company conducts an internal investigation and determines that there is no significant risk of harm resulting from the breach. Each of the bills has slightly different formations of these exceptions to the notice requirement, however.

Law Enforcement Exception

S. 1151 and S. 1408 allow notification to be delayed when either the Secret Service or the FBI determines that providing notification would impede a law enforcement investigation or national security. Notice would be required once law enforcement lifted its security delay.

S. 1535 allows for a similar delay by law enforcement, but this bill would be broader because any federal law enforcement agency or member of the intelligence community may require the delay. The delay in this case may only be accomplished upon written notice from the agency and must specify in writing the period of the delay. This delay may be extended by the law enforcement agency in writing as well. If the delay is not extended, 30 days after the first law enforcement delay order, the entity that experienced the breach would be required to provide notification to individuals whose information was affected.

Risk Assessment Safe Harbor

Businesses and agencies would be exempt from providing notice under all of the bills if they conduct a risk assessment that determines there is no significant risk that the breach will result in certain harms to the individuals affected. The harms the bills are concerned about are similar, but slightly different. S. 1151 and S. 1408 allow for notification to be avoided if no significant risk of identity theft, or physical or economic harm to the individual is found. S. 1535 would allow for avoidance of notification if there is no significant risk of identity theft or physical, economic, or significant emotional harm to the individuals found during the risk assessment.

Under all three bills, the business entity or agency would be required to submit the results of a risk assessment to the FTC and declare its intention to avail itself of the risk assessment safe harbor. The bills would differ slightly on the ways in which the FTC would proceed in granting the exemption, however. Under S. 1151, the FTC, upon receiving the results of a risk assessment, would then indicate in writing that the company or agency may use the safe harbor in order for the exemption from notification to apply. S. 1408, on the other hand, would allow the companies to use the risk assessment safe harbor unless, after notifying the FTC, the FTC indicated in writing that they could not. This would appear to be a broader risk assessment exemption. S. 1535 would require that the agency or business entity consult with the FTC in conducting the risk assessment and that the notification of the entity's intention to use the risk assessment safe harbor be delivered to both the FTC and the designated entity in charge of receiving reports to law enforcement of security breaches. The S. 1535 safe harbor may be used if no significant risk of harm is found and the FTC, or the designated entity, does not indicate that the safe harbor cannot be used, similar to S. 1408.

Each of the bills then would provide for a rebuttable presumption that no significant risk of harm exists if the data subject to the breach were encrypted or rendered otherwise unreadable or indecipherable, which would make it easier for agencies and business entities to avail themselves of the risk assessment safe harbor if they encrypt or otherwise render indecipherable the sensitive, personally identifiable information in their possession. S. 1535 would also create a presumption that there was significant risk of harm due to the breach if the information subject to the breach was not encrypted or otherwise rendered unreadable.

Notice to the Government Regarding a Security Breach

Under all three of the bills, under certain circumstances, entities and agencies experiencing a security breach would be required to notify the federal government of the breach. The bills would require the Secretary of the Department of Homeland Security to designate a central office to receive all notifications regarding security breaches. The bills call that office the "designated entity." That designated entity would then provide notification to the Secret Service, FBI, FTC, and other agencies, as appropriate.

Those experiencing breaches are not always required to notify the government, however. Under S. 1151 and S. 1535, they are only required to notify the government of a breach when the number of individuals affected is greater than 5,000; the database network that was breached contains information regarding 500,000 people, or more, nationwide; or the security breach involved federal government owned databases or involved the sensitive, personally identifiable information of individuals known to be employees or contractors of the government in certain positions. S. 1408 has the same requirements, except companies are not required to notify the government unless the breach pertains to more than 10,000 people, or the breach occurred in a database that held records of more than 1,000,000 people nationwide. Therefore, S. 1408 has a slightly higher threshold for when companies would have to report security breaches to the government. All three bills would require the FTC to conduct a rulemaking regarding what information the chapters of security breaches should contain.

Exemptions from the Notice Requirement

All three bills provide for circumstances in which business entities and agencies would be exempt from providing notice of a security breach entirely. One of the primary reasons for exemptions from the notice requirement is if the entity is already required to provide notification by another federal data security law. All of the bills provide exemptions from the notice requirement for entities to the extent they are financial institutions covered by the security breach notification requirements in the Gramm-Leach-Bliley Act, 15 U.S.C. §§6801 – 6809. The bills would also exempt entities subject to the HIPAA data security provisions, P.L. 104-191 (1996), codified in part at 42 U.S.C. §1320 *et seq.*

All of the bills provide an exemption from the notice requirement for national security reasons. S. 1151 and S. 1535 would provide that if the Secret Service or the FBI determines that providing notification of a breach would reveal methods or sources that would impede law enforcement, notification would not be required. S. 1408 has a similar provision, but it is worded differently. Under that bill, notification would not be required where the Secret Service determined that it could be expected to reveal sensitive sources, law enforcement methods, or otherwise impede law enforcement. The FBI could also prevent notification if the FBI believed such notification would damage national security. In order for the FBI or the Secret Service to prevent disclosure, under S. 1408, the agencies would have to justify the prevention in writing to the Attorney General and the Secretary of DHS, respectively.

The bills also contain an exemption for business entities that participate in a financial fraud security program. If the business entity participates in a security program that effectively blocks the use of sensitive, personally identifiable information to initiate unauthorized financial transactions before the individual's account is charged, and provides notice to the affected person after a breach has resulted in fraud, the notice requirement under these bills would not apply. The notice requirement will apply, however, if the information subject to the breach is more than the individual's credit card number or security code.

Content and Methods of Notice

The bills lay out requirements for providing notification in written, telephone, and public notification formats. However, each bill combines these requirements slightly differently.

Methods of Notification

S. 1151 and S. 1408 would require business entities or agencies to provide individual notice through written notification, telephone notification, or e-mail notification if the individual has consented to receiving notice in that manner. The business entity or agency would also be required to provide notice to state media outlets if the number of residents in that state affected by the breach exceeds 5,000. S. 1408 would include a requirement that when a business entity or agency experiences a breach that affects more than 5,000 people, the agency or entity must notify nationwide consumer reporting as well.

S. 1535 requires more of agencies and businesses that have experienced a breach, however. S. 1535 would require written notice via the physical mail or e-mail, unless the individual has opted out of receiving e-mail. In addition to the written notice, telephone notification would be required as well. If the number of individuals affected by the breach would exceed 5,000, the company or agency must provide notice on its website, and other electronic interfaces, that the breach occurred in addition to the written and telephone notices. Furthermore, like S. 1151 and S. 1408, if an entity or agency experiences a breach that affects more than 5,000 people in a state, then the agency or company must provide notice through major media outlets in the state.

Content of Notification

S. 1151 and S. 1408 would require that notices contain a description of the categories of sensitive information that was or is believed to have been accessed or acquired; a toll free number where affected persons can contact the entity and find out what types of information the entity or agency possessed about that person; as well as contact information for major credit reporting agencies.

States may also require information about that state's victim protection assistance to be included in the notice if the state provides such assistance. The agency or business entity experiencing the breach must also coordinate notification with credit reporting agencies.

S. 1535 is more detailed than the other two bills in its requirements for the content of notifications. The written notice would be required to include a description of the information that had been breached; a toll free number where the individual could obtain information regarding the types of information the entity possesses related to that person; the contact information for credit reporting agencies; phone numbers for federal agencies that provide information about identity theft; and a notification that the person experiencing a breach of their sensitive, personally identifiable information can receive credit reports for two years and credit monitoring that enables the detection of misuse of sensitive, personally identifiable information. The notice must also inform the individual that he or she is entitled to a security freeze. A security freeze would be defined as a notice that prohibits consumer reporting agencies from releasing all or part of an individual's credit report without the consent of the individual, with certain limitations.

Perhaps most importantly, and providing the starkest contrast to the other two bills, the notice required by S. 1535 would also be required to inform the individual that the company or agency providing the notification will be responsible for all costs or damages incurred as a result of the breach. The telephone notification that would be necessary in addition to the written notification would be required to contain notice of the breach and a description of the categories of information that may have been acquired or accessed without authorization. It would also be required to inform individuals of the toll free number where they can obtain further information; the website that may be used to contact the agency or business; a description of the remedies that are available; and a notice that there will be a written notification forthcoming. The public notice that must appear on the company or agency's website will be required to contain notification of the breach, categories of information that were breached, and the toll free number and the website where people can obtain further information. The media notice, if required, must contain everything that must be in the public notice plus the contact numbers for credit reporting agencies; numbers for federal agencies that deal with identity theft; notice that individuals can get free credit reports and monitoring; notice that they are entitled to security freezes; and that the agency or business entity is liable for damages resulting from the breach.

Penalties and Enforcement for Violations of the Notice Requirement

All of the bills would allow the Attorney General and the FTC to enforce violations of the notice requirement with civil penalties resulting from the violations. Their enforcement powers generally and under each of the bills would be slightly different, however.

S. 1151and S. 1408 would allow the Attorney General to bring enforcement actions in federal court against agencies and businesses suspected of violating the notice requirement. Upon proof by a preponderance of the evidence that a violation occurred, the agency or business may be subject to civil penalties of up to $11,000 per day per security breach, with a total fine not to exceed $1,000,000, unless the violation was willful or intentional. If it is shown that the violation was willful or intentional, double penalties up to an additional $1,000,000 may be assessed. The Attorney General may also institute injunctive actions to prevent future violations if it appears that there was an ongoing practice of violation. Similarly, S. 1535 would allow the Attorney General to seek civil penalties of not more than $500 per day per violation, with total penalties not to exceed $20,000, unless the violation was willful. Willful violations would be eligible for higher civil penalties, and certain types of violations would be presumed to be willful. The lower dollar amount for civil penalties under S. 1535 may be due to the fact that S. 1535 makes businesses and agencies financially responsible to individuals for damages done by security breaches. Like S. 1151 and S. 1408, the Attorney General would also be able to obtain injunctions under S. 1535.

S. 1151 and S. 1535 would allow the FTC to enforce violations of the notice requirement as though it were a violation of Section 5 of the FTC Act, 15 U.S.C. §45, because the bills would define violations of the notice requirement as unfair and deceptive trade practices that are prohibited by Section 5. The FTC would also have its various enforcement tools at its disposal, including civil penalties up to $1,000,000, unless the violation were willful in which case double penalties may be awarded.[4] Furthermore the FTC and Attorney General would be required to coordinate their enforcement.

All three of the bills would allow states attorneys general to enforce violations of the notice requirement, under certain circumstances.

Neither S. 1151 nor S. 1408 contain private rights of action. S. 1535 does contain a private right of action, however. Under S. 1535, individuals would be able to sue and obtain damages incurred as a result of violations of the act. They may obtain damages of not more than $500 per individual per day while the violation persists, up to a maximum of $20,000,000 per violation. Punitive damages would also be able to be assessed if the violation were willful. This right of action could not be waived by any agreement or contract between individuals and companies or agencies, and it could not be subject to predispute arbitration agreements. Such requirements would make this a relatively strong private right of action.

Remedies for Security Breach

As noted above, S. 1535 would create the most extensive requirements for the content of the notices to be provided to individuals affected by a security breach. Included in the notice would be the fact that companies and agencies would be liable for any damages or costs to individuals that result from security breaches. Companies and agencies would therefore be liable to individuals for the costs of security breaches under S. 1535. The companies or agencies could comply by providing insurance to the individual against the damages for at least $25,000, or to pay the actual damages and costs. If entities or agencies fail to provide these remedies, they could be subject to private suit by individuals. Damages available would be $500 per day per individual whose information was breached, up to a maximum of $20,000,000 per violation, with punitive damages available for willful violations.

Agencies or business entities would also be required to provide, upon request, consumer credit reports on a quarterly basis for up to two years and credit monitoring, which would help those whose information has been disclosed without authorization detect whether that information is being misused. Individuals may also request a security freeze on their credit reports, which would prevent the release of their credit reports without their express authorization.[5] There would be certain limitations on the prevention of disclosure without consent, as well. The business or agency that experienced the security breach would be responsible for the costs of placing or removing a security freeze.

Data Security Program

S. 1151 and S. 1535 would both require business entities that are involved in collecting, accessing, transmitting, using, storing, or disposing of sensitive, personally identifiable information on 10,000 or more U.S. persons to put a data and privacy security program into place. Business entities would not be required to institute the program if and to the extent that they are in compliance with the requirements of Gramm-Leach-Bliley or HIPAA data security provisions. They would also be exempt from instituting the security program for data they encounter solely in their role as service providers, as defined above.

The data security program would be required to be comprehensive, expanding to the size appropriate for the complexity of each individual business entity and the complexity of the data it is required to protect. The program would have to be designed to ensure privacy, security, and confidentiality, protect against anticipated vulnerabilities, and protect against unauthorized access to the data.

The FTC would be required to conduct a rulemaking to create the administrative, technical, or physical safeguards that would comprise the data security program with which business entities must comply.

Periodic risk assessments would also be required, along with the risk assessments described above that would occur in the event of a security breach. In conducting the assessments, business entities would be required to identify reasonably foreseeable internal and external vulnerabilities that could result in a security breach; assess the likelihood of damage that would result from a breach; assess the sufficiency of its policies to prevent breaches; and assess the vulnerability of sensitive, personally identifiable information during the process of destroying or disposing of such information. The business entity would then be required to design its privacy and security program to control for the risks that it has identified and adopt measures "commensurate with the sensitivity of the data as well as the size, complexity, and scope of the activities of the business entity." This would include program elements that control access to systems and facilities containing protected data; features for detection, recording, and preserving information relevant to actual or attempted unlawful or unauthorized access and disclosure of the protected data; features that protect the data during use, transmission, storage, and disposal that includes encryption; and other protective and preventative measures. Lastly, the business entity would be required to establish a plan and procedure for minimizing the amount of protected data it maintains, by reducing its stores to only that data which is reasonably needed for the business purposes of the entity or to comply with legal obligations.

Each business entity would have to train its employees to comply with these precepts. They would also be required to ensure regular testing of these controls, the frequency of which would be determined by each business entity's risk assessment. In these periodic assessments, the business entity would be required to monitor, evaluate, and adjust its security program as appropriate and in light of relevant changes.

Business entities would also be required to exercise a certain amount of control over third parties when transferring data to them. If the third party would not be covered by the act, the business entity transferring the information would be required to secure the data's security via contractual obligations.

The bills would also create a safe harbor for businesses that comply with or provide protection equal to industry standards or standards widely accepted as an effective industry practice as identified by the FTC.

Penalties and Enforcement

S. 1151 and S. 1535 would create slightly different schemes of penalties and enforcement for violations of the data security program provisions. Under S. 1151, business entities that violate the requirements of the data security program provisions would be subject to civil penalties of not more than $5,000 per violation with a maximum penalty of $500,000, unless the violation is willful or intentional, in which case double penalties may be assessed. Injunctions may also be issued to prevent further violations. The FTC would be given the power to enforce these provisions. States attorneys general would also be given the authority to enforce violations of the data security program requirements in certain circumstances. There is no private cause of action for violations, however.

Under S. 1535, penalties may be slightly more harsh. While singular violations could face civil fines of $5,000 per violation per day, as under S. 1151, the maximum penalty would be raised to $20,000,000, under S. 1535, unless the conduct was willful or intentional. If the violation was willful or intentional, an extra $5,000 per violation per day may be assessed while the violation exists. S. 1535 is also more specific about the considerations to be undertaken when assessing penalties for violations. Like S. 1151, the Attorney General may seek injunctions to prevent future or continuing violations, and states attorneys general may enforce the title as well, under certain circumstances.

Unlike S. 1151, S. 1535 would create a robust private right of action in which any person aggrieved by a violation of the data security program requirements could bring a civil action to recover for the personal injuries the individual sustained as a result of the violation. Remedies could include actual damages of not more than $10,000 per violation per day, up to $20,000,000. Punitive damages could also be assessed if the business entity intentionally and willfully committed the violations. Equitable relief in the form of an injunction would also be available to private litigants. This private right of action would not be able to be waived by the individual via contract with the business entity, nor would predispute arbitration agreements be valid if it would require arbitration of disputes raised by this section.

Preemption

All three bills would preempt all other provisions of federal or state law that relate to notification of security breaches by a business entity engaged in interstate commerce or agencies, with certain exceptions. None of the bills would supersede the data security requirements of the GrammLeach-Bliley Act or any of its implementing regulations. Furthermore, none of the bills would supersede the provisions of Health Information Technology for Economic Clinical Health Act (HITECH Act) which require certain entities to provide breach notifications. S. 1535 also makes clear that it would not preempt state common law, which would mean that businesses would remain liable for state trespasses, contract violations, tort law, and damages caused by a failure to notify an individual following a security breach. S. 1151 would make clear that the bill would not supersede HIPAA privacy provisions, as well.

Reporting on the Use of Exemptions

The bills would also require various reports to Congress. S. 1151 and S. 1535 would require the FTC to report to Congress on the number and nature of the security breaches described in the notices filed by business entities invoking the risk assessment exemption. S. 1535 would require the FBI and the Secret Service to report to Congress on the use of the risk assessment exemption and the response of those agencies to such notices. All three of the bills would require the Secret Service and the FBI to report to Congress on the number and nature of security breaches subject to the national security exemption.

Clearinghouse

S. 1535, unlike the other two bills, would also require the entity designated by the federal government to receive reports of security breaches to create and maintain a clearinghouse of technical information concerning system vulnerabilities identified after security breaches.

Whenever a business entity or agency is required to notify the government of a security breach under the bill, the agency or business entity would also be required to include information about the nature of the breach and vulnerabilities that may have been exposed as a result.

Agencies and business entities may review the information maintained by the clearinghouse for the purposes of preventing security breaches in the future, so long as they obtain certification to access the information. Certification would be obtained from the designated entity, and it would be conditioned on those receiving certification only using the data to improve security, and reduce the vulnerability of networks that use sensitive, personally identifiable information.

The information in the clearinghouse could not be used for competitive commercial purposes and could not be shared with third parties. Furthermore, the data in the clearinghouse would be anonymous to protect those providing data as a result of a breach.

New Crimes and Penalty Enhancements

All three bills would create new crimes for willful concealment of security breaches. Any person who, having knowledge of a security breach that was subject to the notice requirement and that knew the breach was subject to the notice requirement, conceals the security breach, and economic harm results from the breach to any individual in the amount of $1,000 or more, would be guilty of a crime and may be fined, or imprisoned for up to five years, or both.

S. 1151 would add new offenses to the Computer Fraud and Abuse Act (CFAA). It would expand offenses for trafficking in passwords (18 U.S.C. §1030(a)(6)) to cover passwords for access to protected computers, not just government computers.

It would create a new offense for causing or attempting to cause damage to a critical infrastructure computer that results in substantial impairment of the operation of critical infrastructure associated with that computer. Violations could result in fines or imprisonment for between 3 and 20 years, or both. Other amendments to the CFAA would be implemented as well.

Government Contracting Requirements

S. 1535 would also restrict the General Services Administration (GSA) in granting government contracts. Whenever considering a contract award totaling more than $500,000 with data brokers, the GSA would be required to evaluate the data privacy and security program of the data broker, its record of compliance with the program, and its response to security breaches of sensitive, personally identifiable information.

When entering into contracts with data brokers that would involve the use of sensitive, personally identifiable information, the GSA would be required when awarding the contract to attach penalties for failure to comply with the data security and breach notification requirements contained in the bill.

GSA would also have to require data brokers that engage service providers, which are not subject to the data security and notification requirements of the bill, to exercise due diligence in selecting service providers for responsibilities related to sensitive, personally identifiable information; take reasonable steps to select service providers that are capable of maintaining appropriate safeguards; and require the service providers, by contract, to implement and maintain programs designed to meet the objectives of the data security and notification requirements of the bill.

S. 1535 would also amend the Federal Information Security Management Act (44 U.S.C. §3541, *et seq.*) to require agencies implementing information security programs to include procedures for evaluating and auditing the information security practices of contractors and third parties with which the agencies must share sensitive, personally identifiable information.[6]

The agencies would also be required to ensure that remedies will be available should significant deficiencies be discovered in security.

Federal agencies would be prohibited from entering into contracts with data brokers to access for a fee any database containing, primarily, the sensitive, personally identifiable information of U.S. persons, unless the agency has conducted a privacy impact assessment under Section 208 of the E-Government Act of 2002 (44 U.S.C. §3501 note).

Agencies would also have to adopt regulations for fair information practices for databases to be accessed in this manner, and incorporates into contracts with data brokers that are worth more than $500,000 provisions for penalties for failure to comply with the notification requirements of the bill, and penalties for knowingly providing inaccurate sensitive, personally identifiable information to the federal government.

End Notes

[1] The Commercial Law League of America, State Data Security / Breach Notification Laws (as of December 2011), at http://clla.org/. Click "Resources." Click "Data Breach Notification Laws By State." Download document.

[2] For more information about current state and federal data security breach notification laws, see CRS Report R42474, *Selected Federal Data Security Breach Legislation*, by Kathleen Ann Ruane.

[3] For example, S. 1207, the Data Security and Breach Notification Act of 2011 and H.R. 2577, the SAFE Data Act are both bills that would create new federal privacy and security regimes for data.

[4] Beyond seeking civil penalties, the FTC could also seeking injunctive relief, issue cease and desist orders, or institute an administrative procedure against violators of the act. See FTC, A Brief Overview of the FTC's Investigative and Law Enforcement Authority (last revised July, 2008), available at http://www.ftc.gov/ogc/brfovrvw.shtm.

[5] Credit reporting agencies would be entitled to refuse to place or to remove a security freeze from an individual's credit report if the agency determines, in good faith, that the request to place or remove the freeze was part of a fraud.

[6] The bill would specifically amend 44 U.S.C. §3544(b).

In: Data Security Breaches
Editors: P. Diaz and W. C. Long

ISBN: 978-1-62257-735-4
© 2013 Nova Science Publishers, Inc.

Chapter 3

STATEMENT OF DAVID VLADECK, DIRECTOR, BUREAU OF CONSUMER PROTECTION, FEDERAL TRADE COMMISSION. HEARING ON "THE THREAT OF DATA THEFT TO AMERICAN CONSUMERS"[*]

I. INTRODUCTION

Chairman Bono Mack, Ranking Member Butterfield, and members of the Subcommittee, I am David C. Vladeck, Director of the Bureau of Consumer Protection at the Federal Trade Commission ("FTC" or "Commission"). I appreciate the opportunity to present the Commission's testimony on data security.[1]

As the nation's consumer protection agency, the FTC is committed to protecting consumer privacy and promoting data security in the private sector and has brought more than 30 law enforcement actions against businesses that allegedly failed to protect consumers' personal information appropriately, including two new cases yesterday. Data security is of critical importance to consumers. If companies do not protect the personal information they collect and store, that information could fall into the wrong hands, resulting in fraud

---

[*] This is an edited, reformatted and augmented version of testimony presented May 5, 2011 before the House Energy and Commerce Committee.

and other harm, and consumers could lose confidence in the marketplace. Accordingly, the Commission has undertaken substantial efforts to promote data security in the private sector through law enforcement, education, and policy initiatives. And in July, the Commission will be hosting a forum to explore the issue of identity theft targeting children. This testimony provides an overview of the Commission's efforts and reiterates the Commission's unanimous, bipartisan support for legislation that would require companies to implement reasonable security policies and procedures and, in the appropriate circumstances, provide notification to consumers when there is a security breach.

II. THE COMMISSION'S DATA SECURITY PROGRAM

A. Law Enforcement

To promote data security, the Commission enforces several laws and rules that impose obligations upon businesses that possess consumer data. The Commission's Safeguards Rule under the Gramm-Leach-Bliley Act ("GLB Act"), for example, provides data security requirements for financial institutions.[2] The Fair Credit Reporting Act ("FCRA") requires consumer reporting agencies to use reasonable procedures to ensure that the entities to which they disclose sensitive consumer information have a permissible purpose for receiving that information,[3] and imposes safe disposal obligations on entities that maintain consumer report information.[4] In addition, the Commission enforces the FTC Act's proscription against unfair or deceptive acts or practices in cases where a business makes false or misleading claims about its data security procedures, or where its failure to employ reasonable security measures causes or is likely to cause substantial consumer injury.[5]

Since 2001, the Commission has used its authority under these laws to bring 34 cases against businesses that allegedly failed to protect consumers' personal information appropriately.[6] Just yesterday, the Commission announced two new data security cases. The first involves Ceridian Corporation, a large payroll processing company that maintains highly-sensitive payroll information.[7] In December 2009, as a result of Ceridian's alleged failures to adequately protect its data, an intruder was able to hack into Ceridian's payroll processing system and compromise the personal information – including Social Security numbers and financial account numbers – of approximately 28,000 employees of Ceridian's small business customers.

The second case the Commission announced today involves Lookout Services, a company that offers a web-application to assist employers in meeting federal requirements to verify their employees' eligibility to work in the United States.[8] Within this application, Lookout maintains highly-sensitive information provided by employees, including Social Security numbers, dates of birth, passport numbers, alien registration numbers, driver's license numbers, and military identification numbers. In October and December of 2009, due to the company's alleged weak authentication practices and web application vulnerabilities, an employee of a Lookout customer obtained unauthorized access to the entire Lookout customer database.

In both cases, the Commission alleged that the companies did not maintain reasonable safeguards for the highly-sensitive information they maintained. Specifically, the Commission alleged that, among other things, both companies failed to adequately assess the vulnerability of their web applications and networks to commonly known or reasonably foreseeable attacks, such as – in the case of Ceridian – "Structured Query Language" ("SQL") injection attacks and – in the case of Lookout – "predictable resource location," which enables users to easily predict patterns and manipulate the uniform resource locators ("URL") to gain access to secure web pages. The orders require the companies to implement a comprehensive data security program and obtain independent audits for 20 years.

Similarly, earlier this year, the Commission brought actions against three credit report resellers, alleging violations of the FCRA, FTC Act, and the Safeguards Rule.[9] Due to their lack of information security policies and procedures, the respondents in these cases allegedly allowed clients without basic security measures, such as firewalls and updated antivirus software, to access sensitive consumer reports through an online portal. This failure enabled hackers to access more than 1,800 credit reports without authorization. As with *Ceridian* and *Lookout*, the settlements require each company, among other things, to have comprehensive information security programs in place to protect the security, confidentiality, and integrity of consumers' personal information.

B. Education

The Commission also promotes better data security practices through extensive use of consumer and business education. On the consumer education front, the Commission sponsors OnGuard Online, a website designed to educate consumers about basic computer security.[10] OnGuard Online was developed in partnership with other government agencies and the technology sector. Since its launch in 2005, OnGuard Online and its Spanish-language counterpart Alerta en Línea have recorded more than 14 million unique visits.

In addition, the Commission has engaged in wide-ranging efforts to educate consumers about identity theft, one of the harms that could result if their data is not adequately protected.

For example, the FTC's identity theft primer[11] and victim recovery guide[12] are widely available in print and online. Since 2000, the Commission has distributed more than 10 million copies of the two publications and recorded over 5 million visits to the Web versions. In addition, in February 2008, the U.S. Postal Service – in cooperation with the FTC – sent copies of the Commission's identity theft consumer education materials to more than 146 million residences and businesses in the United States. Moreover, the Commission maintains a telephone hotline and dedicated website to assist identity theft victims and collect their complaints, through which approximately 20,000 consumers contact the FTC every week.

The Commission recognizes that its consumer education efforts can be even more effective if it partners with local businesses, community groups, and members of Congress to educate their employees, communities, and constituencies. For example, the Commission has launched a nationwide identity theft education program, "Avoid ID Theft: Deter, Detect, Defend," which contains a consumer education kit that includes direct-to-consumer brochures, training materials, presentation slides, and videos for use by such groups. The Commission has developed a second consumer education toolkit with everything an organization needs to host a "Protect Your Identity Day." Since the campaign launch in 2006, the FTC has distributed nearly 110,000 consumer education kits and over 100,000 Protect Your Identity Day kits.

The Commission directs its outreach to businesses as well. The FTC widely disseminates its business guide on data security, along with an online tutorial based on the guide.[13] These resources are designed to provide diverse businesses – and especially small businesses – with practical, concrete advice as they develop data security programs and plans for their companies. The Commission also has released articles directed towards a non-legal audience regarding basic data security issues for businesses,[14] which have been reprinted in newsletters of local Chambers of Commerce and other business organizations.

The FTC also creates business educational materials on specific topics, often to address emerging issues. For example, last year, the Commission sent letters notifying several dozen public and private entities – including businesses, schools, and local governments – that customer information from their computers had been made available on peer-to-peer ("P2P") file-sharing networks.[15] The purpose of this campaign was to educate businesses and other entities about the risks associated with P2P file-sharing programs and their obligations to protect consumer and employee information from these risks. As part of this initiative, the Commission developed a new business education brochure – *Peer-to-Peer File Sharing: A Guide for Business*.[16] More recently, we issued a guide to businesses about how to properly secure and dispose of information on digital copiers, after news reports called attention to the vast amounts of consumer data remaining on such copiers being prepared for re-sale.[17]

C. Policy

The Commission's efforts to promote data security also include policy initiatives. This testimony describes two such initiatives – the recent Privacy Roundtables and the accompanying preliminary staff report as well as the upcoming forum on child identity theft.

1. Privacy Roundtables and Preliminary Staff Report

In December 2009, February 2010, and March 2010, the FTC convened three public roundtables to explore issues surrounding consumer privacy.[18] Panelists at the roundtables repeatedly noted the importance of data security as an important component of protecting consumers' privacy. Many participants stated that companies should incorporate data security into their everyday business practices, particularly in today's technological age. For example, participants noted the increasing importance of data security in a world where cloud computing enables companies to collect and store vast amounts of data at little cost.[19]

Based on these roundtable discussions, staff issued a preliminary privacy report in December 2010,[20] which proposed and solicited comment on a new framework to guide policymakers and industry as they consider further steps to improve consumer privacy protection. The proposed framework

incorporates the principles of privacy by design, simplifying the presentation of privacy choices for consumers, and improving transparency of privacy practices for consumers. In the context of data security, the principle of "privacy by design" is especially important. Indeed, consumers should not be expected to understand and evaluate the technical details of a company's data security plan; rather, reasonable security should be incorporated into the company's business practices.

As the staff report notes, privacy by design includes several substantive components related to data security. First, companies that maintain information about consumers should employ reasonable safeguards – including physical, technical, and administrative safeguards – to protect that information. The level of security required depends on the sensitivity of the data, the size and nature of a company's business operations, and the types of risks a company faces. Second, companies should collect information only if they have a legitimate business need for it. Because the collection and maintenance of large amounts of data increases the risk of unauthorized access to the data and the potential harm that could result, reasonable data collection practices help support sound data security practices. Third, businesses should retain data only as long as necessary to fulfill the business purposes for which it was collected and should promptly and securely dispose of data for which they no longer have a business need.[21]

While old data may not be valuable to a particular company, it can be highly valuable to an identity thief.

In addition to these substantive principles, the staff report recommends that companies implement and enforce privacy procedures – including appropriate data security – throughout their organizations. This includes assigning personnel to oversee such issues, training employees, and assessing and addressing risks to privacy and security.

2. Child Identity Theft Forum

Along with periodically conducting policy reviews of privacy and security issues generally, the Commission also hosts workshops to study and publicize more specific issues. One such issue that has been in the news recently is identity theft targeting children.[22] For a variety of reasons – including poor safeguards for protecting children's data – identity thieves can get access to children's Social Security numbers. These criminals may deliberately use a child's Social Security number, or fabricate a Social Security number that coincidentally has been assigned to a child, in order to obtain employment,

apply for government benefits, open new accounts, or apply for car loans, or even mortgages. Child identity theft is especially pernicious because the theft may not be detected until the child becomes an adult and seeks employment, or applies for student and car loans.

To address the challenges raised by child identity theft, Commission staff, along with the Department of Justice's Office of Victims of Crime, will host a forum on July 12, 2011. Participants will include educators, child advocates, representatives of various governmental agencies, and the private sector. The forum will include a discussion on how to improve the security of children's data in various contexts, including within the education system as well as the foster care system, where children may be particularly susceptible to identity theft. The goal of the forum is to develop ways to effectively advise parents on how to avoid child identity theft, how to protect children's personal data, and how to help parents and young adults who were victimized as children recover from the crime.

III. DATA SECURITY LEGISLATION

Finally, the Commission reiterates its support for federal legislation that would (1) impose data security standards on companies and (2) require companies, in appropriate circumstances, to provide notification to consumers when there is a security breach.[23] Companies' implementation of reasonable security is important for protecting consumers' data from identity theft and other harm. And if a breach occurs, prompt notification to consumers in appropriate circumstances can mitigate any such harm. For example, in the case of a breach of Social Security numbers, notified consumers can request that fraud alerts be placed in their credit files, obtain copies of their credit reports, scrutinize their monthly account statements, and take other steps to protect themselves.

IV. CONCLUSION

Thank you for the opportunity to provide the Commission's views on the topic of data security. We remain committed to promoting data security and look forward to continuing to work with you on this important issue.

End Notes

[1] This written statement represents the views of the Federal Trade Commission. My oral presentation and responses are my own and do not necessarily reflect the views of the Commission or of any Commissioner.

[2] 16 C.F.R. Part 314, implementing 15 U.S.C. § 6801(b). The Federal Deposit Insurance Corporation, National Credit Union Administration, Securities and Exchange Commission, Office of the Comptroller of the Currency, Board of Governors of the Federal Reserve System, Office of Thrift Supervision, Secretary of the Treasury, and state insurance authorities have promulgated comparable safeguards requirements for the entities they regulate.

[3] 15 U.S.C. § 1681e.

[4] *Id.* at § 1681w. The FTC's implementing rule is at 16 C.F.R. Part 682.

[5] 15 U.S.C. § 45(a).

[6] *See Lookout Servs., Inc.*, FTC File No. 1023076 (May 3, 2011) (consent order approved for public comment); *Ceridian Corp.*, FTC File No. 1023160 (May 3, 2011) (consent order approved for public comment); *SettlementOne Credit Corp.*, FTC File No. 082 3208, *ACRAnet, Inc.*, FTC File No. 092 3088, and *Fajilan & Assocs., Inc.*, FTC File No. 092 3089 (Feb. 3, 2011) (consent orders approved for public comment); *In re Rite Aid Corp.*, FTC File No. 072-3121 (July 27, 2010) (consent order); *In re Twitter, Inc.*, FTC File No. 092-3093 (June 24, 2010) (consent order); *Dave & Buster's, Inc.*, FTC Docket No. C-4291 (May 20, 2010) (consent order); *FTC v. LifeLock, Inc.*, No. 2:10-cv-00530-NVW (D. Ariz. Mar. 15. 2010) (stipulated order); *United States v. ChoicePoint, Inc.*, No. 1:06-CV-0198-JTC (N.D. Ga. Oct. 14, 2009) (stipulated order); *In re James B. Nutter & Co.*, FTC Docket No. C-4258 (June 12, 2009) (consent order); *United States v. Rental Research Servs.*, No. 0:09-CV-00524 (D. Minn. Mar. 6, 2009) (stipulated order); *FTC v. Navone*, No. 2:08-CV-001842 (D. Nev. Dec. 29, 2009) (stipulated order); *United States v. ValueClick, Inc.*, No. 2:08-CV-01711 (C.D. Cal. Mar. 13, 2008) (stipulated order); *United States v. American United Mortg.*, No. 1:07-CV-07064 (N.D. Ill. Dec. 18, 2007) (stipulated order); *In re CVS Caremark Corp.*, FTC Docket No. C-4259 (Jun. 18, 2009) (consent order); *In re Genica Corp.*, FTC Docket No. C-4252 (Mar. 16, 2009) (consent order); *In re Premier Capital Lending, Inc.*, FTC Docket No. C-4241 (Dec. 10, 2008) (consent order); *In re The TJX Cos.*, FTC Docket No. C-4227 (July 29, 2008) (consent order); *In re Reed Elsevier Inc.*, FTC Docket No. C-4226 (July 29, 2008) (consent order); *In re Life is good, Inc.*, FTC Docket No. C-4218 (Apr. 16, 2008) (consent order); *In re Goal Fin'l., LLC*, FTC Docket No. C-4216 (Apr. 9, 2008) (consent order); *In re Guidance Software, Inc.*, FTC Docket No. C-4187 (Mar. 30, 2007) (consent order); *In re CardSystems Solutions, Inc.*, FTC Docket No. C-4168 (Sept. 5, 2006) (consent order); *In re Nations Title Agency, Inc.*, FTC Docket No. C-4161 (June 19, 2006) (consent order); *In re DSW, Inc.*, FTC Docket No. C-4157 (Mar. 7, 2006) (consent order); *In re Superior Mortg. Corp.*, FTC Docket No. C-4153 (Dec. 14, 2005) (consent order); *In re BJ's Wholesale Club, Inc.*, FTC Docket No. C-4148 (Sept. 20, 2005) (consent order); *In re Nationwide Mortg. Group, Inc.*, FTC Docket No. C-9319 (Apr. 12, 2005) (consent order); *In re Petco Animal Supplies, Inc.*, FTC Docket No. C-4133 (Mar. 4, 2005) (consent order); *In re Sunbelt Lending Servs., Inc.*, FTC Docket No. C-4129 (Jan.

3, 2005) (consent order); *In re MTS Inc., d/b/a Tower Records/Books/Video*, FTC Docket No. C-4110 (May 28, 2004) (consent order); *In re Guess?, Inc.*, FTC Docket No. C-4091 (July 30, 2003) (consent order); *In re Microsoft Corp.*, FTC Docket No. C-4069 (Dec. 20, 2002) (consent order).

[7] *Ceridian Corp.*, File No. 1023160 (May 3, 2011) (consent order approved for public comment).

[8] *Lookout Servs., Inc.*, File No. 1023076 (May 3, 2011) (consent order approved for public comment).

[9] *SettlementOne Credit Corp.*, File No. 082 3208; *ACRAnet, Inc.*, File No. 092 3088; *Fajilan and Associates, Inc.*, File No. 092 3089 (Feb. 3, 2011) (consent orders approved for public comment).

[10] *See* www.onguardonline.gov.

[11] *Avoid ID Theft: Deter, Detect, Defend, available at* http://www.ftc.gov/bcp/edu/pubs/consumer/idtheft/idt01.htm.

[12] *Take Charge: Fighting Back Against Identity Theft, available at* http://www.ftc.gov/bcp/edu/pubs/consumer/idtheft/idt04.htm.

[13] *See* www.ftc.gov/infosecurity.

[14] *See* http://business.ftc.gov/privacy-and-security.

[15] *See* FTC Press Release, *Widespread Data Breaches Uncovered by FTC Probe* (Feb. 22. 2010), *available at* www.ftc.gov/opa/2010/02/p2palert.shtm.

[16] *See* http://www.ftc.gov/bcp/edu/pubs/business/idtheft/bus46.shtm.

[17] *See* http://www.cbsnews.com/video/watch/?id=6412572n.

[18] *See generally* FTC Exploring Privacy web page, www.ftc.gov/bcp/workshops/privacy roundtables.

[19] *See, e.g.,* Privacy Roundtable, Transcript of January 28, 2010, at 182, Remarks of Harriet Pearson, IBM (noting the importance of data security as an issue for new computing models, including cloud computing).

[20] *See A Preliminary FTC Staff Report on Protecting Consumer Privacy in an Era of Rapid Change: A Proposed Framework for Businesses and Policymakers* (Dec. 1, 2010), *available at* http://www.ftc.gov/os/2010/12/101201privacyreport.pdf. Commissioners Kovacic and Rosch issued concurring statements available at http://www.ftc.gov/os/2010/12/101201 privacyreport.pdf at Appendix D and Appendix E, respectively.

[21] *See, e.g.,* Privacy Roundtable, Transcript of January 28, 2010, at 310, Remarks of Lee Tien, Electronic Frontier Foundation ("And having the opposite of data retention, data deletion as a policy, as a practice is something that, you know, really doesn't require any fancy new tools. It is just something that people could do, would be very cheap, and would mitigate a lot of privacy problems."); Privacy Roundtable, Transcript of March 17, 2010, at 216, Remarks of Pam Dixon (supporting clear and specific data retention and use guidelines). The Commission has long supported this principle in its data security cases. Indeed, at least three of the Commission's data security cases – against DSW Shoe Warehouse, BJ's Wholesale Club, and Card Systems – involved allegations that companies violated data security laws by retaining magnetic stripe information from customer credit cards much longer than they had a business need to do so. Moreover, in disposing of certain sensitive information, such as credit reports, companies must do so securely. *See* FTC Disposal of Consumer Report Information and Records Rule, 16 C.F.R. § 682 (2005).

[22] *See e.g.,* Richard Power, Carnegie Mellon Cylab, Child Identity Theft, New Evidence Indicates Identity Thieves are Targeting Children for Unused Social Security Numbers (2011), *available at* http://www.cyblog.cylab.cmu.edu/2011/03/child-identity-theft.html; Children's Advocacy Institute, The Fleecing of Foster Children: How We Confiscate Their Assets and Undermine Their Financial Security (2011), *available at* http://www.caichildlaw.org/Misc/Fleecing_Report_Final_HR.pdf.

[23] *See e.g.,* Prepared Statement of the Federal Trade Commission, "Protecting Social Security Numbers From Identity Theft," Before the Subcommittee on Social Security of the House Committee on Ways and Means, 112th Cong., April 13, 2011, *available at* http://ftc.gov/os/

testimony/110411ssn-idtheft.pdf (citing the Commission's support for data security and breach notification standards); FTC, *Security in Numbers, SSNs and ID Theft* (Dec. 2008), *available at* www.ftc.gov/os/2008/12/P075414ssnreport.pdf; and President's Identity Theft Task Force, *Identity Theft Task Force Report* (Sept. 2008), *available at* http://www.idtheft. gov/reports/IDTReport2008.pdf.

In: Data Security Breaches
Editors: P. Diaz and W. C. Long

ISBN: 978-1-62257-735-4
© 2013 Nova Science Publishers, Inc.

Chapter 4

TESTIMONY OF EUGENE H. SPAFFORD, PROFESSOR, PURDUE UNIVERSITY. HEARING ON "THE THREAT OF DATA THEFT TO AMERICAN CONSUMERS"*

SUMMARY OF RECOMMENDATIONS

- A Federal mandatory notification law that includes a requirement for informing consumers about redress should be considered..
- Any regulation or statute should incorporate at least the 24 privacy recommendations listed in Appendix A (the USACM Privacy Principles).
- Any regulation or statute should apply equally to government as well as the private sector to maximize the benefit of development of software, training, and requirements, as well as protection of data.
- Our nation needs to invest in cyber forensic technologies to combat cyber crime, to support law enforcement investigation of data breaches, and to bring criminals to trial.
- Entities holding PII data should be required to meet minimum standards of good security, including staying current with software patches. No particular technology use (e.g., encryption) should be

---

* This is an edited, reformatted and augmented version of testimony presented May 5, 2011 before the House Energy and Commerce Committee.

held out as a "safe harbor"; some form of appropriate third-party standards and audit should be used.

- There should be considerably more support for both fundamental and applied research in privacy and security technologies by both government and the private sector.

- As a nation, we must strengthen the cybersecurity workforce—federal programs should devote resources to improve computer science and computing education programs in K-12 as well as in higher education.

INTRODUCTION

By way of self-introduction, I am a professor at Purdue University. I also have courtesy appointments in the departments of Electrical and Computer Engineering, Philosophy, and Communication. At Purdue, I am also the Executive Director of the Center for Education and Research in Information Assurance and Security (CERIAS). CERIAS is a campus-wide multidisciplinary institute, with a mission to explore important issues related to protecting computing and information resources. We conduct advanced research in several major thrust areas, we educate students at every level, and we have an active community outreach program. CERIAS is the largest such center in the United States, and we have been ranked as the #1 such program in the country. CERIAS also has close working relationships with many of other universities, major commercial firms and government agencies.

Along with my role as an academic faculty member, I have served as an advisor to several Federal agencies, including the FBI, the Air Force, the GAO, and the NSA. I have been working in information security for almost 30 years.

I am also the chair of USACM, the U.S. public policy council of the ACM. With over 100,000 members, ACM is the world's largest educational and scientific computing society, uniting educators, researchers and professionals to inspire dialogue, share resources and address the field's challenges. USACM acts as the focal point for ACM's interaction with the U.S. Congress and government organizations. It seeks to educate and assist policy-makers on legislative and regulatory matters of concern to the computing community. USACM tracks U.S. public policy initiatives that may affect the membership of ACM and the public at large, and provides expert advice to policy-makers. This advice is in the form of nonpartisan scientific data, educational materials, and technical analyses that enable policy-makers to reach better decisions. Members of USACM come from a wide-variety of backgrounds, including industry, academia, government, and end users.

My testimony is as an expert in the field. My testimony does not reflect any official position of Purdue University. My recommendations have been endorsed by USACM.

GENERAL PROBLEM

Citizen concerns about disclosures of personally identifiable information (PII) held in computer databases is not surprising given the significant — and growing — number of reported breaches each year. Organizations are increasingly collecting data about various groups of people and storing that data in computing systems for their use in various business processes — or simply to warehouse for possible future use. However, those systems are often not adequately protected, and portions of the data are exposed by accident or stolen with criminal intent.

Data may be disclosed in a number of ways. Some disclosures are accidental, as a result of carelessness or flaws in the operation of underlying software (or rarely, hardware). Usually, the disclosures are a result of malicious behavior coupled with inadequate protections and policies. Malicious disclosure may come about from authorized employees (insiders) or customers who are taking or disclosing information, usually for financial gain. These disclosures may occur over a long time. These disclosures are often to confederates who commit the crimes using the information, thus making it more difficult to identify the source of the disclosure. The resulting problems may be further complicated by delayed response, and inadequate law enforcement follow-up.

A second form of disclosure occurs when an attacker discovers some flaw or misconfiguration in the system, and uses this to gain access to the desired information. One common current method is via *spear phishing*, which occurs when a targeted piece of attack software is sent in email to a victim inside the target company, masquerading as some harmless document or application from a friend or coworker. When the attack code is run, it acts similar to a virus, installing itself on the local machine, and provides remote access for the criminal to access the system.[1] Similar types of attack code also exist that run from web pages that may be visited by employees of the company.

Attacks can also occur by exploitation of flaws in installed software. For instance, the software that drives a web commerce transaction using the SQL database language may improperly check user input given in response to a question about shipping address. A malicious user may be able to take advantage of this by inserting a semicolon followed by SQL instructions to send the entire customer database over the network to a remote site.

Theft of information is not limited to online copying of data — data exists in physical form as well as online. Thus, the fixed, physical copy can be lost or stolen as well as the online version. There are many documented cases of theft or loss of backup media (disks, tapes, thumb drives, CD-ROMs), theft or loss of laptop computers, and even theft of whole server machines and disks. The theft or loss of paper records may also lead to some of the same forms of disclosure mentioned here — high speed scanners can quickly convert paper documents into database files again; my university has been forced to limit what is printed in our campus phone directory, for instance, because some commercial firms were obtaining copies, digitizing them, and using the results for marketing.

Growth of the Problem

One of the more notable incidents occurred in 2005, when the data broker ChoicePoint revealed that fraudulent access to over 140,000 customer records had occurred over the previous two year period, leading to multiple instances of identity theft and fraud.[2] That incident led to investigations by the FTC and SEC, as well as multiple lawsuits.

Despite the publicity of the ChoicePoint case, and the potential for lessons-learned, the instances of disclosure and loss of PII data have only increased in the years since, with hundreds of cases per year in the United States reported — and undoubtedly many more unreported. This year, before this hearing, two very large and troubling exposures of such data were reported by Sony and Epsilon, with potentially over 100 million consumers affected by the combination of incidents.

These two cases are particularly illustrative of the complexities of such incidents. The individuals affected by the Epsilon case had no idea they had records stored with Epsilon, and likely still have no idea what the extent of their relationship is with that company.[3] In the Sony case, the majority of the victims are likely young people whose sense of risk, privacy and consequence are not yet fully developed, and thus they may also not understand the full ramifications of what has happened. Presumably, both companies are large enough that they could have afforded to spend an appropriate amount on security and privacy protections of their data; I have no information about

what protections they had in place, although some news reports indicate that Sony was running software that was badly out of date, and had been warned about that risk.

To put those incidents in a different perspective, the Privacy Rights Clearinghouse keeps a database[4] of *exposed*[5] breaches from 2005 that includes both accidental disclosures and fraudulent accesses. As of the 1st of May 2011, they documented almost 600 million records have been disclosed in 2,459 separate incidents in the United States. That is an average of approximately 100 million records per year. The Sony breaches disclosed in April and May of 2011 alone equal approximately 100 million records. Other firms listed in their database for those months included Blockbuster, several hospitals, the IEEE (Institute of Electrical and Electronics Engineers) and, a restaurant in southwest Indiana, Albright College in Reading, PA, the Hartford Insurance Company, many doctors offices, US Airways, and Apple iTunes.

Sometimes, a company is involved even though their computers are not the ones breached. Among the more than 50 companies whose customer lists were stolen in the Epsilon data breach were Chase Bank, Hilton, Best Buy, and Target. Customers of those companies should expect to receive emails suggesting that as loyal customers, they can click to receive a valuable coupon. Ironically, some possible fraud may even be in the form of warnings about fraud —customers will receive messages telling them that their email address was stolen and to protect themselves they should click on a link to enter their credit card information, or apologizing for the inconvenience and offering a discount by clicking on a link and signing in, thus disclosing their password to criminals.

It is important to note that data breaches occur in all forms of organizations: retail establishments, financial services, nonprofit entities, health care providers, public utilities, and even computer security firms themselves. Federal and state government agencies are also affected, and are sometimes responsible for disclosure of particularly sensitive material because of their privileged access status under law. A review of the aforementioned list for the last few months reveals disclosures by the IRS, a U.S. District Court, the Social Security Administration, Veterans Affairs, the Oklahoma Department of Health, the Texas Comptroller's Office, the Maine State Prison, and the town of Barton, Vermont (to name a few). Clearly, the problem of properly safeguarding personal information is not limited to the private sector.

Disclosure and theft of PII records has not abated since the ChoicePoint incident in 2005 first prompted Congressional scrutiny. More data is being

collected and stored, often for less well-defined purposes. More firms have access to large-scale storage and computing, and thus are now able to store and aggregate data online. Additionally, there are more entities interested in committing fraud online, and their sophistication and reach has grown considerably faster than has that of law enforcement and security personnel in the same time. Their ability to distribute what they take has also increased with the speed and reach of networks.

Nonetheless, the increase in sophistication of attackers, and the growth in data do not totally explain all the incidents. My personal conclusion from reviews of reports in the press and discussions at professional meetings is that operators of these systems — both in government and the private sector — continue to run outmoded, flawed software, fail to follow some basic good practices of security and privacy, and often have insufficient training or support. The most commonly cited reason for these failings is cost. The cost of providing better security and privacy protection is viewed as overhead that is not recovered in increased revenue, and it is usually one of the first things trimmed in budget cuts. Running outdated software and unpatched operating systems exposes citizens to risks and consequences whose cost a company does not bear. Therefore a company does not have an immediate economic incentive to make the investment needed to prevent breaches. There is a risk of real loss if a breach occurs, however: the cost to a company per record averages $214, and has increased every year since 2005.[6]

As a cautionary note for the future: many companies are eager to move their operations "into the cloud." This will mean that the PII databases may be stored on servers located outside the United States. If those servers are compromised or the media is stolen, it is unclear what legal rights and protections the victims may have.

Types of Abuse

It may not be immediately obvious why disclosure of some of this information might be of concern. In some cases, the disclosure might only be of an account name and some password hint, or directory information that might be otherwise easily found in a public directory. However, such information in context or in combination with other information can be quite.

The presence of a record in a database is informative — that someone is a customer, patient, or subscriber, for instance. Combining information from several different sources may allow someone to infer much more than from any single source alone (and given the availability of information on social media sites and from other breaches, this is not difficult to do).

It is then how these bits of information are used that are of concern. Certainly, any disclosure poses a privacy concern to some users, but there are additional concerns related more specifically to criminal activities.

Identity theft

If sufficient information is obtained about someone, it is often possible to perform identity theft, thus gaining false identification for employment, obtaining credit, or evading law enforcement.

Harassment and stalking

Information about individuals may be used to harass public officials or celebrities, or stalk victims. Obtaining address information may be used to stalk spouses who have fled abuse, for instance.

Spear phishing

Phishing, the attempt to get someone to click through to a false web site through email or divulge their account information, can be made more effective if the email is tailored somewhat to the victim. This is known as spear phishing. Details from large data bases, such as account names, length of service, addresses, and account options can be used to tailor a phishing message to make it appear legitimate and thus trick someone into divulging their account information.

Tracking for physical crime

It is possible to use data from a database to identify victims for physical crime, although I am unaware of any cases of this yet occurring. This would be instances where the database would indicate something about income level or perhaps that indicated people were away on vacation, and this would be useful to criminals seeking to commit burglaries in an area.

Extortion

The presence of information in a database could be used for extortion. This has occurred in cases of medical information, particularly regarding HIV status. There are many other items of information that might be used, including past criminal violations, past marriages, or even items as simple as what videos and on-line books someone likes to download. In an extreme case, some individuals open to extortion might be in sensitive positions, and this could then lead to espionage.

Inference

People tend to use the same passwords, and use the same hints for passwords when visiting multiple sites. The trend at sites to use prompts for password recovery such as "Name your first pet" elicit the same (honest) response from most people or they would otherwise not be able to remember all the answers. Thus, gaining the passwords or hint answers for users from one site might be combined with the same user name at other, more valuable sites such as a bank, to provide access for direct fraud.[7]

Direct fraud

Clearly, information containing credit card numbers, ACH numbers, or other financial information may be used directly — and usually is.

USACM RECOMMENDATIONS

1. **A Federal mandatory notification law that includes a requirement for informing consumers about redress should be considered.** Mandatory notification of consumers after a breach (possibly) involving their PII, along with information about steps to take to safeguard their identity appears to have some positive value. A study[8] by Romanosky, et al. suggests that state mandatory notification laws provide a small decrease (about 6 percent) in identity theft. Not all states have a mandatory notification law.

2. **Any regulation or statute should incorporate at least the 24 privacy recommendations listed in Appendix A.** USACM has developed a set of 24 basic privacy recommendations for use with databases. Those are enclosed as Appendix A to this testimony. We strongly recommend that they be followed for all data sets containing PII, whether government or private, commercial or nonprofit. All of them are important to limit exposure and damage.

3. **Any regulation or statute should apply equally to government as well as the private sector to maximize the benefit of development of software, training, and requirements, as well as protection of**

data. We encourage the committee to ensure that any legislation or regulation apply equally to all government data collections as well as private sector data. The dangers and risks apply no matter who collects and holds collections of PII.

4. **Our nation needs to invest in cyber forensic technologies to combat cyber crime, to support law enforcement investigation of data breaches, and to bring criminals to trial.** Law enforcement also appears to be insufficiently supported with resources for forensic investigation of computing incidents. This is another area where resources for research into better tools and technologies would be helpful. So long as the criminals do not fear apprehension, they will continue to attack our systems. There also appear to be too few agents to investigate breaches, and too few resources to ensure prosecutions.

5. **Entities holding PII data should be required to meet minimum standards of good security, including staying current with software patches. No particular technology use (e.g., encryption) should be held out as a "safe harbor"; some form of appropriate third-party standards and audit should be used.**

6. **There should be considerably more support for both fundamental and applied research in privacy and security technologies by both government and the private sector.** There needs to be additional research into privacy-enhancing and privacy-preservation technologies for large data sets. This is a nascent area of research, as is much of security, and the area is under-resourced. Many of the problems being faced might be solved with better tools, software, and understanding of fundamental processes.

7. **As a nation, we must strengthen the cybersecurity workforce— federal programs should devote resources to improve computer science and computing education programs in K-12 as well as in higher education.** As companies increasingly store data in digital formats, a well-prepared cybersecurity workforce is needed. Strengthening computer science and computing education will help address security challenges in the long-run, ensuring that students have adequate knowledge of the field. The education pipeline feeding our current workforce too often focuses on training rather than education and is frequently absent in K-12 education. Expanding this workforce via education is critical and should start at K-12 and extend through our higher education system.

APPENDIX A. USACM POLICY RECOMMENDATIONS ON PRIVACY

Background

Current computing technologies enable the collection, exchange, analysis, and use of personal information on a scale unprecedented in the history of civilization. These technologies, which are widely used by many types of organizations, allow for massive storage, aggregation, analysis, and dissemination of data. Advanced capabilities for surveillance and data matching/mining are being applied to everything from product marketing to national security.

Despite the intended benefits of using these technologies, there are also significant concerns about their potential for negative impact on personal privacy. Well-publicized instances of personal data exposures and misuse have demonstrated some of the challenges in the adequate protection of privacy. Personal data — including copies of video, audio, and other surveillance — needs to be collected, stored, and managed appropriately throughout every stage of its use by all involved parties. Protecting privacy, however, requires more than simply ensuring effective information security.

The U.S. Public Policy Council of the Association for Computing Machinery (USACM) advocates a proactive approach to privacy policy by both government and private sector organizations. We urge public and private policy makers to embrace the following recommendations when developing systems that make use of personal information. These recommendations should also be central to any development of any legislation, regulations,

international agreements, and internal policies that govern how personal information is stored and managed. Striking a balance between individual privacy rights and valid government and commercial needs is a complex task for technologists and policy makers, but one of vital importance. For this reason, USACM has developed the following recommendations on this important issue.

Recommendations

Minimization

1. Collect and use only the personal information that is strictly required for the purposes stated in the privacy policy.
2. Store information for only as long as it is needed for the stated purposes.
3. If the information is collected for statistical purposes, delete the personal information after the statistics have been calculated and verified.
4. Implement systematic mechanisms to evaluate, reduce, and destroy unneeded and stale personal information on a regular basis, rather than retaining it indefinitely.
5. Before deployment of new activities and technologies that might impact personal privacy, carefully evaluate them for their necessity, effectiveness, and proportionality: the least privacy-invasive alternatives should always be sought.

Consent

6. Unless legally exempt, require each individual's explicit, informed consent to collect or share his or her personal information (*opt-in*); or clearly provide a readily-accessible mechanism for individuals to cause prompt cessation of the sharing of their personal information, including when appropriate, the deletion of that information (*opt-out*). (NB: The advantages and disadvantages of these two approaches will depend on the particular application and relevant regulations.)
7. Whether opt-in or opt-out, require informed consent by the individual before using personal information for any purposes not stated in the privacy policy that was in force at the time of collection of that information.

Openness

8. Whenever any personal information is collected, explicitly state the precise purpose for the collection and all the ways that the information might be used, including any plans to share it with other parties.
9. Be explicit about the default usage of information: whether it will only be used by explicit request (opt-in), or if it will be used until a request is made to discontinue that use (opt-out).

10. Explicitly state how long this information will be stored and used, consistent with the "Minimization" principle.
11. Make these privacy policy statements clear, concise, and conspicuous to those responsible for deciding whether and how to provide the data.
12. Avoid arbitrary, frequent, or undisclosed modification of these policy statements.
13. Communicate these policies to individuals whose data is being collected, unless legally exempted from doing so.

Access

14. Establish and support an individual's right to inspect and make corrections to her or his stored personal information, unless legally exempted from doing so.
15. Provide mechanisms to allow individuals to determine with which parties their information has been shared, and for what purposes, unless legally exempted from doing so.
16. Provide clear, accessible details about how to contact someone appropriate to obtain additional information or to resolve problems relating to stored personal information.

Accuracy

17. Ensure that personal information is sufficiently accurate and up-to-date for the intended purposes.

18. Ensure that all corrections are propagated in a timely manner to all parties that have received or supplied the inaccurate data.

Security

19. Use appropriate physical, administrative, and technical measures to maintain all personal information securely and protect it against unauthorized and inappropriate access or modification.
20. Apply security measures to all potential storage and transmission of the data, including all electronic (portable storage, laptops, backup media), and physical (printouts, microfiche) copies.

Accountability

21. Promote accountability for how personal information is collected, maintained, and shared.
22. Enforce adherence to privacy policies through such methods as audit logs, internal reviews, independent audits, and sanctions for policy violations.
23. Maintain *provenance* — information regarding the sources and history of personal data — for at least as long as the data itself is stored.
24. Ensure that the parties most able to mitigate potential privacy risks and privacy violation incidents are trained, authorized, equipped, and motivated to do so.

USACM does not accept the view that individual privacy must typically be sacrificed to achieve effective implementation of systems, nor do we accept that cost reduction is always a sufficient reason to reduce privacy protections. Computing options are available today for meeting many private sector and government needs while fully embracing the recommendations described above. These include the use of de-identified data, aggregated data, limited datasets, and narrowly defined and fully audited queries and searches. New technologies are being investigated and developed that can further protect privacy. USACM can assist policy-makers in identifying experts and applicable technologies.

(June 2006)

End Notes

[1] There have been some very high-profile cases of spear phishing in the news recently. Oak Ridge National Labs had to shut down their Internet connection in April when over 500 employees were attacked like this, RSA had some of their security software compromised this spring via spear phishing, and the highly publicized breakins of Google and over 30 other large companies were accomplished with spear phishing from China.

[2] See "The ChoicePoint Dilemma", by Paul N. Otto, Annie I. Antón, and David L. Baumer, *IEEE Security & Privacy*, Sep/Oct 2007, pp. 15-23.

[3] This is similar to the ChoicePoint breach in that the individuals affected in that incident also did not realize the relationship they had with the company.

[4] Available at http://www.privacyrights.org/data-breach#CP

[5] I emphasize *exposed* because there are undoubtedly many more that are undisclosed, and many that are also simply not discovered. There may be more that are undiscovered than disclosed and undisclosed combined.

[6] According to an annual study by the Ponemon Institute: http://www.ponemon.org/blog/post/ cost-of-a-data-breach-climbs-higher

[7] See, for example, http://www.pcworld.com/article/188763/too_many_people_reuse_logins_ study_finds.html or http://www.lightbluetouchpaper.org/2011/02/09/measuring-password-re-use-empirically/

[8] Romanosky, Sasha, Telang, Rahul and Acquisti, Alessandro, Do Data Breach Disclosure Laws Reduce Identity Theft? (Updated) (September 16, 2008). Forthcoming in the Journal of Policy Analysis and Management, 2011. Available at SSRN: http://ssrn.com/abstract= 1268926

In: Data Security Breaches
Editors: P. Diaz and W. C. Long

ISBN: 978-1-62257-735-4
© 2013 Nova Science Publishers, Inc.

Chapter 5

IDENTITY THEFT: TRENDS AND ISSUES*

Kristin M. Finklea

SUMMARY

In the current fiscal environment, policymakers are increasingly concerned with securing the economic health of the United States—including combating those crimes that threaten to further undermine the nation's financial stability. Identity theft is one such crime. In 2010, about 8.1 million Americans were reportedly victims of identity fraud, and the average identity fraud victim incurred a mean of $631 in costs as a result of the fraud—the highest level since 2007. Identity theft is often committed to facilitate other crimes such as credit card fraud, document fraud, or employment fraud, which in turn can affect not only the nation's economy but its security. Consequently, in securing the nation and its economic health, policymakers are also tasked with reducing identity theft and its impact.

Identity theft has remained the dominant consumer fraud complaint to the Federal Trade Commission (FTC). Nevertheless, while the number of overall identity theft complaints generally increased between when the FTC began

---

* This is an edited, reformatted and augmented version of the Congressional Research Service Publication, CRS Report for Congress R40599, dated February 15, 2012.

recording identity theft complaints in 2000 and 2008, the number of complaints decreased in both 2009 and 2010. Prosecutions of federal identity theft violations have followed a similar pattern. However, while the number of identity theft cases filed and the number of defendants convicted both decreased in FY2009 and FY2010 relative to FY2008, the numbers of *aggravated* identity theft cases filed and defendants convicted have continued to increase.

Congress continues to debate the federal government's role in (1) preventing identity theft and its related crimes, (2) mitigating the potential effects of identity theft after it occurs, and (3) providing the most effective tools to investigate and prosecute identity thieves. With respect to preventing identity theft, one issue concerning policymakers is the prevalence of personally identifiable information—and in particular, the prevalence of Social Security numbers (SSNs)—in both the private and public sectors. One policy option to reduce their prevalence may involve restricting the use of SSNs on government-issued documents such as Medicare identification cards. Another option could entail providing federal agencies with increased regulatory authority to curb the prevalence of SSN use in the private sector. In debating policies to mitigate the effects of identity theft, one option Congress may consider is whether to strengthen data breach notification requirements. Such requirements could affect the notification of relevant law enforcement authorities as well as any individuals whose personally identifiable information may be at risk from the breach. Congress may also be interested in assessing the true scope of data breaches, particularly involving government networks (e.g., S. 2105).

There have already been several legislative and administrative actions aimed at curtailing identity theft. Congress enacted legislation naming identity theft as a federal crime in 1998 (P.L. 105-318) and later provided for enhanced penalties for aggravated identity theft (P.L. 108-275). In April 2007, the President's Identity Theft Task Force issued recommendations to combat identity theft, including specific legislative recommendations to close identity theft-related gaps in the federal criminal statutes. In a further attempt to curb identity theft, Congress directed the FTC to issue an Identity Theft Red Flags Rule (effective December 31, 2010), requiring that creditors and financial institutions with specified account types develop and institute written identity theft prevention programs.

INTRODUCTION

In the current fiscal environment, policymakers are increasingly concerned with securing the economic health of the United States—including combating those crimes that threaten to further undermine the nation's financial stability.[1] Identity theft, for one, poses both security and economic risks. By some estimates, identity fraud cost Americans $37 billion in 2010.[2] FTC complaint data indicate that the most common fraud complaint received (19% of all consumer fraud complaints) is that of identity theft.[3] In 2010, for instance, about 8.1 million Americans were reportedly victims of identity fraud. This is a decrease of about 3 million from the approximately 11.1 million who were victimized in 2009.[4] Despite this decline in the overall number of reported identity fraud incidents, difficulty in detecting and resolving these incidents may have contributed in higher consumer costs; the average identity fraud victim incurred a mean of $631—the highest level since 2007.[5]

An increase in globalization and a lack of cyber borders provide an environment ripe for identity thieves to operate from within the nation's borders—as well as from beyond. Federal law enforcement is thus challenged with investigating criminals who may or may not be operating within U.S. borders; may have numerous identities—actual, stolen, or cyber; and may be acting alone or as part of a sophisticated criminal enterprise.[6] In addition, identity theft is often interconnected with various other criminal activities. These activities range from credit card and bank fraud to immigration and employment fraud. In turn, the effects felt by individuals and businesses who have fallen prey to identity thieves extend outside of pure financial burdens; identity thieves affect not only the nation's economic health, but its national security as well. Consequently, policymakers may debate the federal government's role in preventing identity theft and its related crimes, mitigating the potential effects of identity theft after it occurs, and providing the most effective tools to investigate and prosecute identity thieves.

This chapter first provides a brief federal legislative history of identity theft laws. It analyzes the current trends in identity theft, including prevalent identity theft-related crimes, the federal agencies involved in combating identity theft, and the trends in identity theft complaints and prosecutions. The chapter also discusses the relationship between data breaches and identity theft as well as possible effects of the FTC's Identity Theft Red Flags Rule, effective December 31, 2010. It also examines possible issues for Congress to consider.

DEFINITIONS OF IDENTITY THEFT

When does taking and using someone else's identity become a crime? Current federal law defines identity theft as a federal crime when someone

> knowingly transfers, possesses, or uses, without lawful authority, a means of identification of another person with the intent to commit, or to aid or abet, or in connection with, any unlawful activity that constitutes a violation of Federal law, or that constitutes a felony under any applicable State or local law.[7]

The current federal law also provides enhanced penalties for aggravated identity theft when someone "knowingly transfers, possesses, or uses, without lawful authority, a means of identification of another person" in the commission of particular felony violations.[8] Aggravated identity theft carries an enhanced two-year prison sentence for most specified crimes and an enhanced five-year sentence for specified terrorism violations.

Identity theft is also defined in the Code of Federal Regulations (CFR) as "fraud committed or attempted using the identifying information of another person without permission."[9] Identity theft can both facilitate and be facilitated by other crimes. For example, identity theft may make possible crimes such as bank fraud, document fraud, or immigration fraud, and it may be aided by crimes such as theft in the form of robbery or burglary.[10] Therefore, one of the primary challenges in analyzing the trends in identity theft (e.g., offending, victimization, or prosecution rates)—as well as the policy issues that Congress may wish to consider—arises from this interconnectivity between identity theft and other crimes.

Theft vs. Fraud

Identity theft and identity fraud are terms that are often used interchangeably. Identity fraud[11] is the umbrella term that refers to a number of crimes involving the use of false identification— though not *necessarily* a means of identification belonging to another person. Identity theft is the specific form of identity fraud that involves using the personally identifiable information of someone else. Both identity fraud and identity theft are crimes often committed in connection with other violations, as mentioned above. Identity theft, however, may involve an added element of victimization, as this form of fraud may directly affect the life of the victim whose identity was stolen in addition to defrauding third parties (such as the government, employers, consumers, financial institutions, and health care and insurance providers, just to name a few). This chapter, however, maintains a focus on identity theft rather than the broader term of identity fraud.

Knowledge Element

Another definitional issue is one that was recently before the U.S. Supreme Court. The statutory definitions of identity theft and aggravated identity theft indicate that they are crimes when someone "*knowingly* transfers, possesses, or uses, without lawful authority, a means of identification of another person" in conjunction with specified felony violations outlined in the U.S. Code. The definitional element under question was the word "knowingly." In *Flores-Figueroa v. United States*, the Court decided that in order to be found guilty of aggravated identity theft, a defendant must have knowledge that the means of identification he used belonged to another individual.[12] It is not sufficient to only have knowledge that the means of identification used was not his own. Although the case before the Court specifically involved aggravated identity theft, the issue may apply to the identity theft statute as well, due to its overlap in wording about the element of knowledge.

Since the Court has issued its final decision in *Flores-Figueroa v. United States*, Congress may wish to consider whether there is a need to clarify the difference between these two types of knowledge in the U.S. Code. If a clarification is warranted, Congress may wish to consider whether the identity theft and aggravated identity theft statutes should be amended to reflect the definitions of both types of knowledge.

LEGISLATIVE HISTORY[13]

Until 1998, identity theft was not a federal crime.[14] Leading up to Congress designating identity theft as a federal crime, identity fraud was on the rise, and the Internet was increasingly being used as a method of defrauding innocent victims. Law enforcement and policymakers suggested that the current laws at the time were ineffective at combating the growing prevalence of identity theft;[15] the laws were not keeping up with technology, and stronger laws were needed to investigate and punish identity thieves.[16] In addition, policymakers also suggested that industries that handled records containing individuals' personally identifiable information—such as credit, medical, and criminal records—needed superior methods to ensure the validity of the information they collected and utilized.

Identity Theft Assumption Deterrence Act

In 1998, Congress passed the Identity Theft Assumption Deterrence Act (P.L. 105-318), which criminalized identity theft at the federal level. In addition to making identity theft a crime, this act provided penalties for individuals who either committed or attempted to commit identity theft and provided for forfeiture of property used or intended to be used in the fraud. It also directed the Federal Trade Commission (FTC) to record complaints of identity theft, provide victims with informational materials, and refer complaints to the appropriate consumer reporting and law enforcement agencies. The FTC now records consumer complaint data and reports it in the Identity Theft Data Clearinghouse; identity theft complaint data are available for 2000 and forward.[17]

Identity Theft Penalty Enhancement Act

Congress further strengthened the federal government's ability to prosecute identity theft with the passage of the Identity Theft Penalty Enhancement Act (P.L. 108-275).[18] This act established penalties for *aggravated identity theft*, in which a convicted perpetrator could receive additional penalties (two to five years' imprisonment) for identity theft committed in relation to other federal crimes. Examples of such federal crimes include theft of public property, theft by a bank officer or employee, theft from employee benefit plans, false statements regarding Social Security and Medicare benefits, several fraud and immigration offenses, and specified felony violations pertaining to terrorist acts.

Identity Theft Enforcement and Restitution Act of 2008

Most recently, Congress enhanced the identity theft laws by passing the Identity Theft Enforcement and Restitution Act of 2008 (Title II of P.L. 110-326). Among other elements, the act authorized restitution to identity theft victims for their time spent recovering from the harm caused by the actual or intended identity theft.

IDENTITY THEFT TASK FORCE

In addition to congressional efforts to combat identity theft, there have been administrative efforts as well. The President's Identity Theft Task Force (Task Force) was established in May 2006 by Executive Order 13402.[19] The task force was created to coordinate federal agencies in their efforts against identity theft, and it was charged with creating a strategic plan to combat (increase awareness of, prevent, detect, and prosecute) identity theft. It was composed of representatives from 17 federal agencies.[20]

Recommendations

In April 2007, the task force authored a strategic plan for combating identity theft in which it made recommendations in four primary areas:

- preventing identity theft by keeping consumer data out of criminals' hands,
- preventing identity theft by making it more difficult for criminals to misuse consumer data,
- assisting victims in detecting and recovering from identity theft, and
- deterring identity theft by increasing the prosecution and punishment of identity thieves.[21]

With respect to identity theft prevention, the task force suggested that decreasing the use of Social Security numbers (SSNs) in the public sector and reviewing the use of SSNs in the private sector could help prevent identity theft. Also, the task force suggested that educating employers and individuals on how to safeguard data, as well as establishing national data protection and breach notification standards, could further aid in preventing identity theft.

Relating to victim assistance, the task force suggested that identity theft victims may be better served if first responders were specially trained to assist this particular class of victim. It also addressed victim redress by recommending that identity theft victims be able to obtain an alternative identification document after the theft of their identities. Through the Identity Theft Enforcement and Restitution Act of 2008 (Title II of P.L. 110-326), Congress responded to the task force's recommendation that criminal restitution statutes allow victims to be compensated for their time in recovering from the actual or attempted identity theft.

Regarding identity theft deterrence, the task force recommended enhancing information gathering and sharing between domestic law enforcement agencies and the private sector, ramping up identity theft training for law enforcement and prosecutors, and increasing enforcement and prosecution of identity theft. The task force also promoted international cooperation to decrease identity theft through identifying countries that may be safe havens for identity thieves, encouraging anti-identity theft legislation in other countries, and increasing international cooperation in the investigation and prosecution of identity theft.

Legislative Recommendations

More specifically, the task force recommended that Congress close gaps in the federal criminal statues to more effectively prosecute and punish identity theft-related offenses by

- amending the identity theft and aggravated identity theft statutes so that thieves who misappropriate the identities of corporations and organizations—and not just the identities of individuals—can be prosecuted,
- amending the aggravated identity theft statute by adding new crimes as predicate offenses for aggravated identity theft violations,
- amending the statute criminalizing the theft of electronic data by eliminating provisions requiring that the information be stolen through interstate communications,
- amending the computer fraud statute by eliminating the requirement that damage to a victim's computer exceed $5,000,

- amending the cyber-extortion statute by expanding the definition of cyber-extortion, and
- ensuring that the Sentencing Commission allows for enhanced sentences imposed on identity thieves whose actions affect multiple victims.[22]

Congress has already taken steps to address some of these task force recommendations. Through the Identity Theft Enforcement and Restitution Act of 2008 (Title II of P.L. 110-326), Congress, among other things, eliminated provisions in the U.S. Code requiring the illegal conduct to involve interstate or foreign communication, eliminated provisions requiring that damage to a victim's computer amass to $5,000, and expanded the definition of cyber-extortion.

However, Congress has not yet addressed the task force recommendation to expand the identity theft and aggravated identity theft statutes to apply to corporations and organizations as well as to individuals, nor has it addressed the recommendation to expand the list of predicate offenses for aggravated identity theft. Issues surrounding these recommendations are analyzed in the section "Potential Issues for Congress."

RED FLAGS RULE[23]

The Identity Theft Red Flags Rule, issued in 2007, requires creditors and financial institutions to implement identity theft prevention programs. It is implemented pursuant to the Fair and Accurate Credit Transactions (FACT) Act of 2003 (P.L. 108-159). The FACT Act amended the Fair Credit Reporting Act (FCRA)[24] by directing the FTC, along with the federal banking agencies and the National Credit Union Administration, to develop Red Flags guidelines. These guidelines require creditors[25] and financial institutions[26] with "covered accounts"[27] to develop and institute written identity theft prevention programs. According to the FTC, the identity theft prevention programs required by the rule must provide for

- identifying patterns, practices, or specific activities—known as "red flags"—that could indicate identity theft and then incorporating those red flags into the identity theft prevention program;
- detecting those red flags that have been incorporated into the identity theft prevention program;

- responding to the detection of red flags; and
- updating the identity theft prevention program periodically to reflect any changes in identity theft risks.[28]

Possible "red flags" could include

- alerts, notifications, or warnings from a consumer reporting agency;
- suspicious documents;
- suspicious personally identifiable information, such as a suspicious address;
- unusual use of—or suspicious activity relating to—a covered account; and
- notices from customers, victims of identity theft, law enforcement authorities, or other businesses about possible identity theft in connection with covered accounts.[29]

The deadline for creditors and financial institutions to comply with the Red Flags Rule was originally set at November 1, 2008. However, many of the organizations affected by the Red Flags Rule were not prepared to institute their identity theft prevention programs by this date. Therefore, the FTC moved the deadline to May 1, 2009,[30] further extended the compliance date to November 1, 2009,[31] and later to June 1, 2010.[32] The final enforcement date was set at December 31, 2010,[33] and this last extension was, in part, a result of the debate over whether Congress wrote the FACT Act Red Flags provision too broadly by including all entities qualifying as creditors and financial institutions (discussed further below).

The effect that the Red Flags Rule will have on the prevalence of identity theft remains uncertain. One potential effect is that the Red Flags Rule may help creditors and financial institutions prevent identity theft by identifying potential lapses in security or suspicious activities that could lead to identity theft. This could possibly lead to an overall decrease in the number of identity theft incidents reported to the FTC, as well as the number of identity theft cases investigated and prosecuted. Once detected, the Red Flags Rule requires that the creditor or financial institution respond to the identified red flag. One response option that creditors and financial institutions might include in their prevention programs is to notify consumers or law enforcement of data breaches that could potentially lead to the theft of consumers' personally identifiable information. While notification is not a required element in the identity theft prevention programs,[34] early notification could lead to consumers taking swift action to prevent identity theft or mitigate the severity of the damage that could result if they had not been notified as quickly.

When the Red Flags Rule was created, the FTC originally estimated that it would impact approximately 11.1 million creditors and financial institutions required to implement the identity theft prevention programs.[35] The FTC estimated the total annual labor costs (for each of the first three years the rule is in effect) for all creditors and financial institutions covered by the rule to be about $143 million.[36] Some entities considered creditors or financial institutions under the rule expressed concern that the burden of the rule overlaps with burdens already incurred under other regulations. For example, the American Bar Association (ABA) questioned whether lawyers are considered "creditors" under the Red Flags Rule because they generally do not require payment until after services are rendered. Further, the American Medical Association indicated that physicians should be exempt from the Red Flags Rule because of patient privacy and security protections required by the Health Insurance Portability and Accountability Act (HIPAA).[37] In addition, there may have been concern that to avoid being considered creditors, some physicians could possibly require full payment at the time of service (rather than allowing deferred payments). This could in turn lead to some patients avoiding potentially necessary treatment if they are unable to pay in full at the time of service; on the other hand, the rule may have no effect on patients' willingness to seek medical treatment. The Red Flag Program Clarification Act of 2010 (P.L. 111-319), signed by President Obama on December 18, 2010, limits the Red Flags Rule's definition of a creditor, excluding any creditor "that advances funds on behalf of a person for expenses incidental to a service provided by the creditor to that person." This legislation does not exempt any broad categories of businesses or entities, but the majority of businesses in certain categories—such as physicians—would be exempt from Red Flags Rule compliance. The actual effects of the Red Flags Rule—including effects on identity theft rates as well as any indirect consequences—will not be evident until after full implementation by creditors and financial institutions. Congress may consider monitoring the effects of the impending Red Flags Rule on subsequent identity theft rates.

TRENDS IN IDENTITY THEFT

As previously mentioned, research indicates that in 2010, about 8.1 million Americans were victims of identity theft. This is a decrease of about 3 million from the approximately 11.1 million who were victimized in 2009.[38] Consumer complaints of identity theft to the FTC exhibited a corresponding decrease. The FTC received 250,854 consumer complaints of identity theft in 2010, down from 278,356 complaints in 2009. However, identity theft incidents reported to the FTC remain a fraction of the estimated victim population. There is a noted difference between the 250,854 complaints received by the FTC in 2010 and survey data indicating that about 8.1 million people were actually victimized. This disparity between research on identity theft victimization and consumer reports could be a result of several factors. For one, while some identity theft victims may file a report with the FTC, others may file complaints with credit bureaus, while still others may file complaints with law enforcement. Not all victims, however, may file complaints with consumer protection entities, credit reporting agencies, and law enforcement. Another possible factor contributing to the disparity is that victims may not—for any number of reasons— report an identity theft incident. These individuals, however, may be more likely to indicate the incident on a survey prompting them about their experiences with identity theft or fraud.

Since the FTC began recording consumer complaint data in 2000, identity theft has remained the most common consumer fraud complaint. Figure 1 illustrates the number of identity theft complaints received by the FTC between 2000 and 2010 in relation to the number of all other fraud complaints received. According to CRS analysis, since 2000, the number of identity theft complaints has averaged about 35% of the total number of consumer complaints received by the FTC.[39]

Identity theft has remained the dominant consumer fraud complaint to the FTC. However, while the number of overall identity theft complaints generally increased between 2000 (when the commission began recording identity theft complaints) and 2008, the number of complaints decreased in both 2009 and 2010. Figure 2 illustrates these trends in identity theft complaints reported to the FTC.

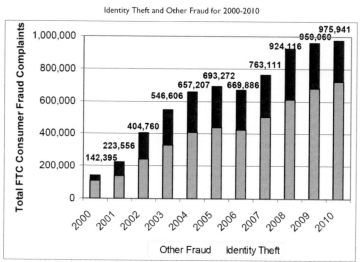

Figure 1. FTC Consumer Complaint Data.

Source: CRS presentation of FTC Identity Theft Clearinghouse data. Annual reports for each calendar year are available at http://www.ftc.gov/sentinel/reports/sentinel -annual-reports/sentinel-cy2010.pdf.

Notes: Data indicate the number of identity theft and other fraud complaints received by the FTC each calendar year. According to CRS analysis, between 2000 and 2010, the number of identity theft complaints has averaged about 35% of the total number of consumer complaints received by the FTC. The percentage has ranged between about 22% and about 40%.

Perpetrators

Increasing globalization and the expansion of the Internet have provided a challenging environment for law enforcement to both identify and apprehend identity thieves targeting persons residing in the United States. For one, these criminals may be operating from within U.S. borders as well as from beyond. There is no publically available information, however, delineating the proportion of identity theft (or other crimes known to be identity theft-related) committed by domestic and international criminals.[40] Secondly, while some identity thieves operate alone, others operate as part of larger criminal networks or organized crime syndicates. The FBI has indicated that it, for one, targets identity theft investigations on larger criminal networks.[41] These criminal networks may involve identity thieves located in various cities across the United States or in multiple cities around the world, and these criminals may be victimizing not only Americans, but persons living in countries across the globe. In a joint study by Verizon and the U.S. Secret Service of selected data breaches of businesses around the globe during 2010, 58% of data breaches by "external agents"—sources outside the compromised organization— were attributed to organized crime.[42] It is unknown, however, how many of these records compromised by organized crime were used in identity theft and related crimes. A third challenge in identifying identity thieves is that perpetrators may operate under multiple identities including actual identities, various stolen identities, and cyber identities and nicknames.

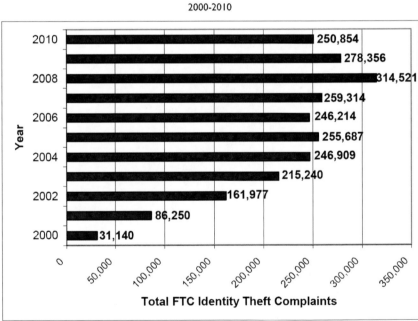

Source: CRS presentation of FTC Identity Theft Clearinghouse data. Annual reports for each calendar year are available at http://www.ftc.gov/sentinel/reports/ sentinel-annual-reports/sentinel-cy2010.pdfl.

Notes: Data indicate the number of identity theft complaints received by the FTC each calendar year.

Figure 2. FTC Identity Theft Complaint Data.

Investigations and Prosecutions

As mentioned earlier, identity theft is defined broadly, and it is directly involved in a number of other crimes and frauds. As a result, there are practical investigative implications that influence analysts' abilities to understand the true extent of identity theft in the United States. For instance, only a proportion (the exact number of which is unknown) of identity theft incidents are reported to law enforcement. While some instances may be reported to consumer protection agencies (e.g., the FTC), credit reporting agencies (e.g., Equifax, Experian, and Trans Union), and law enforcement agencies, some instances may be reported to only one. For example, the FTC indicates that of the 42% of identity theft complaints that included information on whether the theft was reported to law enforcement, 72% were reported to law enforcement.[43]

Another issue that may affect analysts' abilities to evaluate the true extent of identity theft is that law enforcement agencies may not uniformly report identity theft because crime incident reporting forms may not necessarily contain specific categories for identity theft. In addition, there may not be standard procedures for recording the identity theft component of the criminal violations of primary concern.[44] Issues such as these may lead to discrepancies between data available on identity theft reported by consumers, identity theft reported by state and local law enforcement, and identity theft investigated and prosecuted by federal law enforcement.

Various federal agencies are involved in investigating identity theft, including the Federal Bureau of Investigation (FBI), the United States Secret Service (USSS), the United States Postal Inspection Service (USPIS), the Social Security Administration Office of the Inspector General (SSA OIG), and the U.S. Immigration and Customs Enforcement (ICE). In addition, federal law enforcement agencies may work on task forces with state and local law enforcement as well as with international authorities to bring identity thieves to justice. The Department of Justice (DOJ) is responsible for prosecuting federal identity theft cases.

Federal Bureau of Investigation (FBI)

The FBI investigates identity theft primarily through its Financial Crimes Section. However, because the nature of identity theft is cross-cutting and may facilitate many other crimes, identity theft is investigated in other sections of the FBI as well. The FBI is involved in over 20 identity theft task forces and working groups around the country. It is also involved in over 80 other financial crimes task forces, which may also investigate cases with identity theft elements.[45] The FBI focuses its identity theft crime fighting resources on those cases involving organized groups of identity thieves and criminal enterprises that affect a large number of victims.[46] The FBI partners with the National White Collar Crime Center (NW3C) to form the Internet Crime Complaint Center (IC3). The IC3 serves the broad law enforcement community to receive, develop, and refer Internet crime complaints—including those of identity theft.[47] In 2010, 9.8% of all Internet crime complaints received by the IC3 were that of identity theft.[48] However, other complaint categories such as credit card fraud may have involved incidents of identity theft as well.

United States Secret Service (USSS)

The USSS serves a dual mission of (1) protecting the nation's financial infrastructure and payment systems to safeguard the economy and (2) protecting national leaders.[49] In carrying out the former part of this mission, the USSS conducts criminal investigations into counterfeiting, financial crimes, computer fraud, and computer-based attacks on the nation's financial and critical infrastructures. The Secret Service has 38 Financial Crimes Task Forces and 31 Electronic Fraud Task Forces that investigate identity theft, as well as a number of other crimes.[50] In FY2010, the Secret Service arrested 4,040 suspects for crimes related to identity theft, and in FY2011, they arrested 4,570 such suspects.[51]

United States Postal Inspection Service (USPIS)

The USPIS is involved in inter-agency task forces investigating identity theft and is the lead federal investigative agency when identity thieves have used the postal system in conducting their fraudulent activities. The most recent USPIS data indicate that in FY2010, the USPIS participated in 18 identity theft task forces, and postal inspectors arrested 759 identity theft suspects—from both USPIS investigations and task force investigations in which the USPIS was involved.[52] In addition to investigating identity theft, the USPIS has been involved in delivering educational presentations to consumer groups to assist in preventing identity theft, and inspectors are involved in sponsoring outreach programs for victims of identity theft; in FY2010, they provided 667 cases of identity theft victim assistance.[53] Examples of victim services include notifying victims of potential identity theft if the USPIS discovers compromised identities as well as assisting in victim restitution by providing victims money from the funds forfeited as a result of USPIS identity theft investigations.[54]

Social Security Administration Office of the Inspector General (SSA OIG)

Because the theft and misuse of Social Security numbers (SSNs) is one of the primary modes of identity theft, the SSA OIG is involved in investigating identity theft. The SSA has programs to assist victims of identity theft who have had their SSNs stolen or misused by placing fraud alerts on their credit files, replacing Social Security cards, issuing new Social Security numbers in specific instances, and helping to correct victims' earnings records.[55] The SSA OIG protects the integrity of the SSN by investigating and detecting fraud, waste, and abuse. It also determines how the use or misuse of SSNs influences programs administered by the SSA. The SSA OIG is involved in providing a limited range of SSN verification for law enforcement agencies. Further, the SSA OIG maintains a hotline for consumers to report identity theft, and then these data are transferred to the FTC to be included in their consumer complaint database.[56]

Immigration and Customs Enforcement

The U.S. Immigration and Customs Enforcement (ICE) investigates cases involving identity theft, particularly immigration cases that involve document and benefit fraud. In FY2008, ICE conducted 3,636 investigations of document and benefit fraud. In addition, it made 1,652 criminal arrests and seized about $10.3 million related to document and benefit fraud.[57] In 2006, ICE created Document and Benefit Fraud Task Forces (DBFTFs). These DBFTFs, located in 18 cities throughout the United States, are aimed at dismantling and seizing the financial assets of criminal organizations that threaten the nation's security by engaging in document and benefits fraud.

Department of Justice

The U.S. Attorneys Offices (USAOs) prosecute federal identity theft cases referred by the various investigative agencies. CRS was unable to determine the proportion of identity theft cases referred to the USAOs by each investigative agency for several reasons. For one, some of the investigations reported by each agency are investigations conducted by a task force, to which several agencies may have contributed. Consequently, these investigations may be reported by each participating agency. If the total number of reported investigations from each agency were combined, it is likely that the overall number of identity theft investigations would be inflated because of double (or more) reporting of an investigation from multiple agencies. A second factor is that the USAOs do not track the proportion of case referrals by statute; rather, they track case referrals by program area. For instance, the proportion of identity theft (18 U.S.C. §1028) and aggravated identity theft (18 U.S.C. §1028A) case referrals from each agency are not tracked according to the charging statutes. Identity theft cases fall under several programmatic categories—including white collar crime and immigration—which also contain several other crimes. Thus, trends in federal identity theft and aggravated identity theft cases may be better tracked by the number of total cases referred to and prosecuted by the USAOs, irrespective of the referring agency.

Somewhat mirroring the trend in identity theft complaints reported to the FTC, there was a recent decrease in the number of identity theft cases prosecuted by DOJ. Figure 3 illustrates the number of identity theft (18 U.S.C. §1028) and aggravated identity theft (18 U.S.C. §1028A) cases filed (specifically, the number of *defendant* cases filed[58]) with the USAOs as well as defendants convicted between FY1998 and FY2010.

While the number of identity theft cases filed and the number of defendants convicted both decreased in FY2009 and FY2010 relative to FY2008, the numbers of aggravated identity theft cases filed and defendants convicted have continued to increase. Still, if the identity theft and aggravated identity theft data are combined, total case filings and prosecutions both decreased in FY2009 and FY2010. There are several possible explanations for these trends. One possibility is that there has been a decrease in the overall number of identity theft incidents, and law enforcement has been responding proportionally by arresting fewer identity thieves and filing fewer cases with the U.S. Attorneys' Offices. While the decrease in the number of identity theft complaints to the FTC, as reflected in Figure 2, suggests that this may be a viable explanation, some research indicates that the number of individuals victimized by identity thieves is actually continuing to increase.[59] A second possibility is that there has actually been an increase in the number of identity theft incidents, but that either these criminals are evading federal law enforcement or law enforcement has dedicated fewer resources toward combating identity theft, which has resulted in decreased investigations and prosecutions. Yet another explanation may be that fewer perpetrators are actually impacting a greater number of victims. As criminals become more technologically savvy, they may be able to expand their reach to a greater number of victims.

Defendant Cases Filed and Defendants Convicted FY1998-FY2010

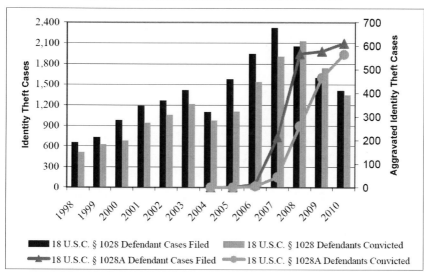

Source: CRS analysis of data provided by the USAO, Congressional Affairs.

Notes: Identity theft defendant cases filed and convictions are plotted on the left Y-axis while the aggravated identity theft cases filed and convictions are plotted on the right Y-axis. Identity theft is prosecuted under 18 U.S.C. §1028 and aggravated identity theft is prosecuted under 18 U.S.C. §1028A. Identity theft became a federal crime in 1998, and aggravated identity theft became a federal crime in 2004. Data include all cases filed with the USAOs containing an identity theft or aggravated identity theft violation, and are not limited to those cases where identity theft or aggravated identity theft is the lead charge. This includes data filed with the USAOs from all federal agencies.

Figure 3. Federal Identity Theft and Aggravated Identity Theft Cases.

As illustrated in Figure 3, the number of identity theft cases filed in FY2010 maintained the downward trend from FY2008 and FY2009. This was accompanied by a sustained increase in aggravated identity theft case filings. Several factors could possibly contribute to these divergent trends. One explanation is that some cases in which defendants would have been charged with identity theft in earlier years may more recently have resulted in defendants being charged with aggravated identity theft. Therefore, a decrease in identity theft case filings may be complemented with an increase in aggravated identity theft case filings. As mentioned before, aggravated identity theft became a federal crime in 2004, and is reflected in Figure 3 by the increase in aggravated identity theft case filings and convictions in later years.

Analysts would need to evaluate several more years of data to make any reliable or valid predictions regarding factors contributing to fluctuations in identity theft and aggravated identity theft prosecutions.

Domestic Impact

As mentioned, in 2010, about 8.1 million Americans were reportedly victims of identity fraud.[60] And these are the known cases. The Federal Trade Commission (FTC) recognizes two primary forms of identity theft: existing account fraud and new account fraud. Existing account fraud refers to the misuse of a consumer's existing credit card, debit card, or other account, while new account fraud refers to the use of stolen consumer identifying information to open new accounts in the consumer's name.[61] Figure 4 illustrates the most common misuses of victims' identities.

Between 2000—when the FTC began tracking identity theft complaints— and 2008, the FTC consistently reported that the most common misuse of a victim's identity was credit card fraud.[62] In 2008, government documents and benefits fraud became the second most prevalent misuse of a victim's identity, and in 2010, it became the most prevalent.[63] Within the documents/benefits fraud category, the FTC has reported a particularly large increase in identity theft related to tax return fraud. And, tax return-related fraud was involved in about 15.5% of the identity theft complaints received by the FTC in 2010.[64]

Identity theft and the various crimes it facilitates affect the economy and national security of the United States. Selected crimes facilitated by identity theft are outlined in the section below.

Credit Card Fraud[65]

After a victim's identity is stolen, the primary criminal use of this information is credit card fraud. Beyond amassing charges on a victim's credit card, identity thieves may sometimes change the billing address so that the victim will not receive the bills and see the fraudulent charges, allowing the thief more time to abuse the victim's identity and credit. If a victim does not receive the bill, and therefore does not pay it, this could aversely affect the victim's credit. In addition to abusing existing credit card accounts, a thief could also open new accounts in the victim's name, incurring more charges on the victim's line of credit. These actions could in turn affect not only the victim's immediate pocketbook, but future credit as well. The Identity Theft Resource Center (ITRC) has predicted that organized crime groups will become more involved in identity theft-related crime such as credit card fraud and that these crimes will become increasingly transnational.[66] As mentioned, criminals are no longer constrained by physical borders, and they can victimize U.S. persons and businesses both from within the United States and from beyond.

How Victims' Information is Misused

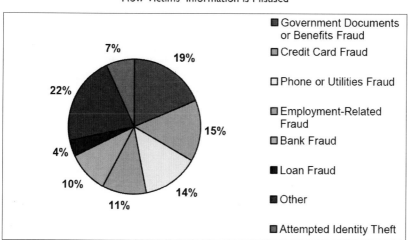

Source: FTC Identity Theft Clearinghouse data, *Consumer Sentinel Network Data Book for January - December 2010,* March 2011, http://www.ftc.gov/sentinel/ reports/sentinel-annual-reports/sentinel-cy2010.pdf.

Notes: Of the 250,854 identity theft complaints received by the FTC in 2010, the most prevalent form of identity theft was government documents or benefits fraud. About 12% of the identity theft complaints received by the FTC involved more than one form of identity theft. For this reason, the sum of the various types of identity theft included in the figure amounts to greater than 100%. Also, within in the category "other," are complaints of victims' identities being misused across subcategories including evading the law, medical, Internet/e-mail, apartment/house rented, insurance, securities/other investments, property rental fraud, magazines, child support, bankruptcy, miscellaneous, and uncertain. The uncertain subcategory alone accounts for about 9% of all identity theft complaints.

Figure 4. FTC Identity Theft Complaints, 2010.

- In February 2011, Operation Power Outage led to the arrest of 83 individuals associated with Armenian Power, an Armenian and Eastern European transnational criminal organization. These individuals were allegedly involved in a range of criminal activities including credit card fraud. One scheme is reported to have used skimming devices, secretly installed on cash register machines, to steal customer account information. This information was subsequently used tocreate counterfeit credit and debit cards.[67]

Document Fraud[68]

Identity thieves can use personally identifiable information to create fake or counterfeit documents such as birth certificates, licenses, and Social Security cards. One way that thieves can use the stolen information is to obtain government benefits in a victim's name. This directly affects the victim if the victim attempts to legitimately apply for benefits and then is denied because someone else may already be (fraudulently) receiving those benefits under the victim's name. The creation of fraudulent documents may, among other things, provide fake identities for unauthorized immigrants[69] living in the United States or fake passports for people trying to illegally enter the United States. In addition, DOJ has indicated that identity theft is implicated in international terrorism. In May 2002, former Attorney General John Ashcroft stated that

> [I]dentity theft is a major facilitator of international terrorism. Terrorists have used stolen identities in connection with planned terrorist attacks. An Algerian national facing U.S. charges of identity theft, for example, allegedly stole the identities of 21 members of a health club in Cambridge, Massachusetts, and transferred the identities to one of the individuals convicted in the failed 1999 plot to bomb the Los Angeles International Airport.[70]

Identity theft and resulting document fraud can thus have not only an economic impact on the United States, but a national security impact as well.

- In November 2011, at least 25 individuals were indicted for their alleged roles in large-scale fraudulent document manufacturing rings. Individuals produced fraudulent documents such as Legal Permanent Resident cards, Social Security cards, Mexican Consular

Identification cards, and driver's licenses. These fraudulent documents reportedly supported a variety of criminal activities such as credit and bank fraud, tax fraud, identity theft, and pharmaceutical diversion schemes.[71]

Employment Fraud

Identity theft can facilitate employment fraud if the thief uses the victim's personally identifiable information to obtain a job. With the currently elevated level of unemployment,[72] policymakers may wish to monitor trends in employment fraud. This form of fraud could aversely affect a victim's credit, ability to file his or her taxes, and ability to obtain future employment, among other things. Not only can identity theft lead to employment fraud, but employment fraud may be a means to steal someone's identity. Identity thieves may use scams that falsely advertise employment as a means to phish for personally identifiable information. The thief can then use this information to commit other crimes while the job-seeking individual remains unemployed and victimized.

DATA BREACHES AND IDENTITY THEFT

As mentioned, the number of identity theft complaints reported to the FTC generally increased through 2008 and then declined in 2009 and 2010. The number of reported data breaches followed a similar trend, despite a divergence in 2010. The Identity Theft Resource Center (ITRC) tracks data breaches across the nation, and the resulting statistics indicate that the total number of reported data breaches generally increased between 2005 and 2010, with the only decline in 2009.[73] Figure 5 illustrates this trend. The IRTC indicates that the number of data breaches increased from 158 in 2005 to 662 in 2010. Breaches are recorded across five industries: banking/credit/financial, business, education, government/military, and medical/healthcare. In 2010, the business industry experienced the greatest number of data breaches (42.1%), followed by healthcare (24.2%) and government/military (15.7%).[74]

Several factors may influence the number of reported breaches. One such factor may be the increasing number of states that have enacted laws requiring data breach notification.[75] California was the first state to enact such legislation in 2002. As of October 2010, 46 states, the District of Columbia,

Puerto Rico, and the U.S. Virgin Islands have enacted data breach notification laws.[76] The increasing prevalence of state laws requiring breach notification could lead to an increase in reported breaches to law enforcement, media, or the individuals affected. This could lead to an increase in the reported number of data breaches captured by the ITRC. Nonetheless, the actual number of data breaches remains underreported, and the number of breaches does not reflect the magnitude of data breaches. Because of these factors, analysts are unable to say with certainty whether the increase in the number of reported data breaches in 2010 is an accurate reflection of the trend in data breaches.

Furthermore, the number of records affected by each data breach is variable, and in many cases unknown. In 2010, for example, at least 16,167,542 records were put at risk, but information on the exact number of records exposed was only available for 338 (about 51%) of the 662 reported data breaches.[77]

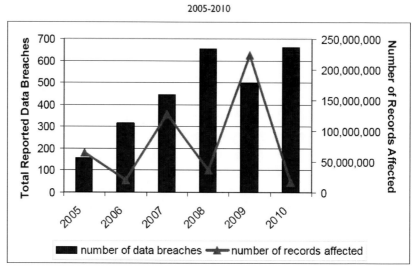

Source: CRS analysis of data provided by the Identity Theft Resource Center, available at http://www.idtheftcenter.org/artman2/publish/lib_survey/ITRC_2008_Breach_List.shtml#.

Notes: Breaches are recorded across five primary industries: banking/credit/financial, business, educational, government/military, and medical/healthcare.

Figure 5. Total Number of Reported Data Breaches and Records Affected.

Because available data on known data breaches and reported identity theft incidents are not comprehensive, and because year-to-year changes in one measure may not trend with changes in the other, it can be difficult to determine whether there is a relationship between the two. Intuitively, the data breaches and identity theft may seem to correlate, but some analysts have found that the link may not be very strong. There are several ways to analyze the relationship between data breaches and identity theft. One is to examine the set of data breach victims and determine the proportion of those victims that are also victims of identity theft. Some claim that data breaches are a direct cause of identity theft and may rely on this position to advocate the need for increased data security and data breach notification laws to protect consumers and help with quickly mitigating any potential damage from such data breaches. Meanwhile, other experts claim that less than 1% of data breach victims are also victims of identity theft.[78] Some may use this data to argue against the need for increased data security and breach notification laws, suggesting that such laws could produce a larger cost for businesses than prevention for consumers. In 2010, 7% of U.S. consumers received notification of a data breach. And, Javelin Strategy and Research data suggest that individuals receiving breach notifications "had more than four times higher risk of identity fraud than did those who didn't receive these types of notifications."[79]

Another means to evaluate the relationship between data breaches and identity theft is to examine identity theft victims and analyze the proportion of those victims whose identity was stolen as a result of a data breach. Javelin Strategy and Research (2009) found that about 11% of victims' identities that were stolen had been under the control of a company and were stolen from the company through methods such as data breaches. Most victims (65%) did not know how their identities had been stolen, and some proportion of these could have occurred as a result of a data breach.[80] Synovate (2007) conducted a similar study on behalf of the Federal Trade Commission and found that about 12% of victims' stolen identities had been under the control of a company and were thus accessed via a data breach.[81] The Center for Identity Management and Information Protection at Utica College (2007) evaluated identity theft cases handled by the U.S. Secret Service between 2002 and 2006 and found that in nearly 27% of the cases, a breach of company-controlled data was the source of the identity theft.[82]

It appears that the stronger relationship between identity theft and data breaches is found when analyzing identity theft victims whose data were obtained through a data breach rather than in analyzing data breaches that result in identity theft. In efforts to curb identity theft, policymakers are left with the issue of how to target data breaches. The question is whether the federal government's role in curbing identity theft should be more preventative, more responsive, or both. One policy option may be for Congress to increase data security for the purpose of preventing those data breaches that could potentially result in identity theft. Congress has already enacted data breach laws targeting certain components of the public and private sectors, such as the Veterans Administration and healthcare providers.[83] Another option could be for Congress to dedicate resources to assisting victims of identity theft and providing sufficient deterrence and punishment measures (in the form of penalties or sanctions). These options are analyzed further below.

POTENTIAL ISSUES FOR CONGRESS

As Congress debates means to prevent identity theft, mitigate the potential effects of identity theft, and investigate and prosecute identity thieves, there are several issues policymakers may wish to consider. One issue surrounds the extent to which reducing the availability of SSNs may reduce the prevalence of identity theft. A second issue involves the degree to which increasing breach notification requirements may reduce both identity theft and the monetary burden incurred by victims. Yet another issue concerns the adequacy of (1) the current legal definitions of identity theft and aggravated identity theft and (2) the list of predicate offenses for aggravated identity theft.

Identity Theft Prevention

Policymakers may question what the extent of the federal government's role should be in preventing identity theft. One element of this discussion centers around the fact that identity theft is often committed to facilitate other crimes and frauds (e.g., credit card fraud, document fraud, and employment fraud). Consequently, preventing identity theft could proactively prevent other crimes. When policymakers consider the federal government's role in preventing identity theft, they necessarily consider the government's role in preventing interrelated crimes.

Congress may also consider the various means available to prevent identity theft and evaluate the federal government's role—if any—in implementing them. Possible ways to prevent identity theft include securing data in the private sector, securing data in the public sector, and improving consumer authentication processes.[84]

Securing Social Security Numbers

The prevalence of personally identifiable information—and in particular, of Social Security numbers (SSN)—has been an issue concerning policymakers, analysts, and data security experts.[85] There are few restrictions on the use of SSNs in the private sector, and therefore the use of SSNs is widespread.[86] Some industries, such as the financial services industry, have stricter requirements for safeguarding personally identifying information. There are greater restrictions on the use of SSNs in the public sector, as Congress has already taken direct steps in reducing the prevalence of SSNs in this arena. For example, in the Intelligence Reform and Terrorism Prevention Act of 2004 (P.L. 108-458), Congress prohibited states from displaying or electronically including SSNs on driver's licenses, motor vehicle registrations, or personal identification cards. One document that continues to display SSNs, however, is the Medicare identification card. Congress may consider whether the continued display of SSNs on Medicare cards places individuals at undue risk for identity theft as well as for becoming a victim of other crimes facilitated by identity theft and whether it should enact legislation to prohibit the display of SSNs on Medicare cards. Proponents of legislation to remove SSNs from Medicare cards cite reports that as of 2007, 42 million Medicare cards displayed Social Security numbers, potentially placing these individuals at risk for identity theft.[87] Opponents of such legislation may cite that transitioning to a different Medicare identifier has been estimated to cost more than $300 million.[88]

Another policy option to safeguard personally identifiable information that Congress may consider is increasing restrictions on the disclosure of certain forms of personally identifiable information, such as SSNs, in connection with federally funded grant programs. One example of Congress taking such action is in the Violence Against Women and Department of Justice Reauthorization Act of 2005 (P.L. 109-162). Provisions in this act prohibit grantees that receive funds under the Violence Against Women Act of 1994 from disclosing certain personally identifiable information—including SSNs—collected in connection with services through the grant program.[89] Congress may consider whether existing SSN restrictions for federal grant recipients are sufficient or whether the federal government should play a larger role in limiting the use of SSNs—and more specifically, whether it should set limitations as part of eligibility requirements for federal assistance.

The Government Accountability Office (GAO) has identified vulnerabilities in federal laws protecting personally identifiable information—and specifically, SSNs—across industries. For one, some industries, such as the financial services industry, have more restrictions on safeguarding this information, while information resellers are not covered by the same restrictions.[90] In order to reduce discrepancies across industries, one policy option may be to provide certain federal agencies with authority to curb the prevalence of SSN use in the private sector; for example, the GAO has recommended that Congress provide the SSA with the authority to enact standards for uniformly truncating SSNs so that the entire nine-digit numbers are not as readily available.[91] A similar option may be to provide the Attorney General, the FTC, or the SSA with the authority to set rules and standards for the sale and purchase of SSNs.

Others have suggested that policies should be focused on *eliminating* the use of SSNs as authenticators rather than on *securing* their use. The premise is that SSNs are often public information and, if not already available, they can be predicted with relative ease.[92] For instance, researchers have demonstrated how the public availability of names and birth data allow for SSN predictability and subsequent vulnerability. As such, some have recommended that efforts not be focused on securing SSNs that are often already public and predictable. Rather, they have suggested that private sector entities abandon the SSN in favor of an alternative identity authenticator.[93]

Effects of Data Breaches

One issue that Congress may consider involves the relationship between data breaches and identity theft. Although there is not a large body of research examining this relationship, existing data suggest that between 12%[94] and 27%[95] of identity theft incidents may result from data breaches. However, this proportion is truly unknown because most victims of identity theft do not know precisely how their personally identifiable information was acquired. In order to prevent any proportion of identity theft that may result from data breaches, or to mitigate the extent of the damage resulting from breach-related identity theft, Congress may wish to consider whether to strengthen data breach notification requirements. Such requirements could affect both the notification of the relevant law enforcement authorities as well as the notification of the individual whose personally identifiable information may be at risk from the breach.

Proponents of increasing breach notification requirements point to research on recent trends in identity theft and the resulting monetary loss. As mentioned, the sooner people become aware that they are victims of identity theft, the faster they take compensatory steps to mitigate the damage.[96] Proponents also argue that placing enhanced reporting requirements on industries may influence businesses to increase their data security standards, which could, in effect, decrease data breaches and any possibly resulting identity theft.[97] On the other hand, opponents of increasing notification requirements point to research suggesting that the percentage of data breaches that result in identity theft could be less than 1%, as previously discussed.[98] Opponents may then argue that the costs that businesses could incur from increased notification (in terms of dollars and personnel time) could thus exceed the costs incurred by potential identity theft victims from the small proportion of data breaches that may actually result in identity theft.

In addition to strengthening post-breach notification requirements, another policy option aimed at decreasing data breach-related identity theft involves strengthening data security. Several options to reduce the availability of personally identifiable information were discussed in the preceding section. However, a broader data security issue concerns overall information security. Because many incidents of identity theft may occur over the Internet, enhancing cyber security measures could reduce the incidents of identity theft.[99]

Deterrence and Punishment

As mentioned, identity theft is broadly defined in current law. This is in part because it is a facilitating crime, and the criminal act of stealing someone's identity often does not end there. Consequently, investigating and prosecuting identity theft often involves investigating and prosecuting a number of related crimes. In light of this interconnectivity, the President's Identity Theft Task Force recommended expanding the list of predicate offenses for aggravated identity theft, as discussed earlier.[100] The task force specifically suggested adding identity theft-related crimes such as mail theft,[101] counterfeit securities,[102] and tax fraud.[103] However, the task force did not cite specific data to support the claim that these specifically mentioned crimes are in fact those most often related to (either facilitating or facilitated by) identity theft. If Congress considers expanding the list of predicate offenses for aggravated identity theft, it may request that the U.S. Attorneys as well as the appropriate investigative agencies (e.g., FBI, USSS, ICE, and USPIS) provide a report detailing the relationship between identity theft and other federal crimes not yet codified as predicate offenses. A second question that Congress may raise if it considers expanding the list of predicate offenses regards which identity theft-related crimes may most affect national priorities such as economic health and national security.

As more information is stored online by individuals and organizations, there is a risk that online identity thieves may take advantage of this large body of data. And there need not be an increasing number of data breaches in order for criminals to reach a large pool of information. For instance, while the number of reported data breaches decreased in 2009, the number of records impacted spiked over previous years, as illustrated in Figure 5. As mentioned, the range of potential victims includes not only individuals but organizations as well. The task force cites "phishing" as a means by which identity thieves assume the identity of a corporation or organization in order to solicit personally identifiable information from individuals.[104] For reasons such as this, the task force recommended that Congress clarify the identity theft and aggravated identity theft statutes to cover both individuals and organizations targeted by identity thieves.

SELECTED LEGISLATION FROM THE 112TH CONGRESS

Several pieces of legislation introduced in the 112th Congress would address the trends in identity theft. The proposals would provide for measures to safeguard information and persons possibly at risk for identity theft.

Social Security Numbers

Legislation was proposed to secure Social Security numbers (SSNs) as well as to minimize the public availability of these numbers. Proposals include prohibiting the display of SSNs on Medicare, Medicaid, or Children's Health Insurance Plan (CHIP) identification cards.[105] Other proposals would require the Commissioner of Social Security to issue a new SSN to a child whose account number has been stolen.[106] Policymakers also proposed legislation to prevent unauthorized access to information contained in the Social Security Death Master File.[107]

Legislation was introduced that would require the Attorney General and the Comptroller General to report to Congress on the uses of Social Security numbers as well as the prevalence of Social Security numbers in public records.[108]

Law Enforcement and Consumer Notification

Legislation introduced in the 112th Congress would enhance both law enforcement and consumer notification of suspected identity theft. For example, some proposals would require the Secretary of the Treasury to notify the FBI as well as the potential victim if there is substantial likelihood that the individual's social security account number was fraudulently used in the employment context.[109] Still others would require the agency or business entity wherein a data breach occurred to notify law enforcement, the FTC, and the individuals whose personally identifiable information may have been compromised.[110]

End Notes

[1] See, for example, U.S. Congress, House Committee on Ways and Means, *Role of Social Security Numbers in Identity Theft and Options to Guard Their Privacy*, 112th Cong., 1st sess., April 13, 2011.

[2] Javelin Strategy & Research, *2011 Identity Fraud Survey Report: Consumer Version*, February 2011.

[3] Federal Trade Commission, *Consumer Sentinel Network Data Book for January–December, 2010*, March, 2011,http://www.ftc.gov/sentinel/reports/sentinel-annual-reports/sentinel-cy2010.pdf.

[4] Javelin Strategy & Research, *2011 Identity Fraud Survey Report: Consumer Version*, February 2011.

[5] Ibid.

[6] For more information on these challenges, see CRS Report R41927, *The Interplay of Borders, Turf, Cyberspace, and Jurisdiction: Issues Confronting U.S. Law Enforcement*, by Kristin M. Finklea.

[7] 18 U.S.C. §1028(a)(7).

[8] These felony violations as outlined in 18 U.S.C. §1028A include theft of public money, property, or records; theft, embezzlement, or misapplication by bank officer or employee theft from employee benefit plans; false personation of citizenship; false statements in connection with the acquisition of a firearm; fraud and false statements; mail, bank, and wire fraud; specified nationality and citizenship violations; specified passport and visa violations; obtaining customer information by false pretenses; specified violations the

Immigration and Nationality Act relating to willfully failing to leave the United States after deportation and creating a counterfeit alien registration card and various other immigration offenses; specified violations of the Social Security Act relating to false statements relating to programs under the act; and specified terrorism violations. The basic penalty for identity theft under 18 U.S.C. §1028 ranges from not more than five years imprisonment to not more than 30 years, depending on the circumstances.

[9] According to the CFR definitional section for the Fair Credit Reporting Act (16 C.F.R. §603.2), "[t]he term "identifying information" means any name or number that may be used, alone or in conjunction with any other information, to identify a specific person, including any— (1) Name, Social Security number, date of birth, official State or government issued driver's license or identification number, alien registration number, government passport number, employer or taxpayer identification number; (2) Unique biometric data, such as fingerprint, voice print, retina or iris image, or other unique physical representation; (3) Unique electronic identification number, address, or routing code; or (4) Telecommunication identifying information or access device (as defined in 18 U.S.C. 1029(e))."

[10] Graeme R. Newman and Megan M. McNally, "Identity Theft Literature Review," Prepared for presentation and discussion at the National Institute of Justice Focus Group Meeting to develop a research agenda to identify the most effective avenues of research that will impact on prevention, harm reduction and enforcement, Contract #2005-TO-008, January 2005, http://www.ncjrs.gov/pdffiles1/nij/grants/210459.pdf.

[11] Identity fraud became a federal crime through the False Identification Crime Control Act of 1982 (P.L. 97-398), and it is codified at 18 U.S.C. §1028.

[12] *Flores-Figueroa v. United States*, 129 S. Ct. 1186 (2009).

[13] The legislation described in this section covers those Acts directly related to the identity theft statutes. Other statutes, such as the credit reporting statutes, indirectly address identity theft by possibly assisting victims, however, they are not discussed here. For more information on the scope of federal laws relating to identity theft, see archived CRS ReportRL31919, *Federal Laws Related to Identity Theft*, by Gina Stevens. See also CRS Report RL31666, *Fair Credit Reporting Act: Rights and Responsibilities*, by Margaret Mikyung Lee.

[14] The first state to enact an identity theft law was Arizona in 1996.

[15] Before identity theft became a federal crime, identity fraud had been established as a crime in the False Identification Crime Control Act of 1982 (P.L. 97-398). However, the identity fraud statute did not contain a specific theft provision.

[16] From remarks James Bauer, Deputy Assistant Director, Office of Investigations, U.S. Secret Service, before the U.S. Congress, Senate Committee on the Judiciary, Subcommittee on Technology, Terrorism, and Government Information, *The Identity Theft and Assumption Deterrence Act*, 105th Cong., 2nd sess., May 20, 1998.

[17] Unless otherwise noted in this chapter, all dates refer to calendar years rather than fiscal years.

[18] Aggravated Identity Theft is codified at 18 U.S.C. §1028A.

[19] Executive Order 13402, "Strengthening Federal Efforts To Protect Against Identity Theft," 71 *Federal Register* 93, May 15, 2006.

[20] Members of the task force included the Attorney General (chair), the Chairman of the Federal Trade Commission (co-chair), the Secretary of the Treasury, the Secretary of Commerce, the Secretary of Health and Human Services, the Secretary of Veterans Affairs, the Secretary of Homeland Security, the Director of the Office of Management and Budget, the Commissioner of Social Security, the Chairman of the Board of Governors of the Federal Reserve System, the Chairperson of the Board of Directors of the Federal Deposit Insurance Corporation, the Comptroller of the Currency, the Director of the Office of Thrift Supervision, the Chairman of the National Credit Union Administration Board, the Postmaster General, the Director of the Office of Personnel Management, and the Chairman of the Securities and Exchange Commission.

[21] The President's Identity Theft Task Force, *Combating Identity Theft: A Strategic Plan*, April 23, 2007, at http://www.identitytheft.gov/reports/StrategicPlan.pdf.

[22] Ibid.

[23] The Red Flags Rule is listed in the Code of Federal Regulations at 16 C.F.R. §681.2. The Red Flags Rule was issued jointly by the FTC; the Office of the Comptroller of the Currency, Treasury; the Board of Governors of the Federal Reserve System; the Federal Deposit Insurance Corporation; the Office of Thrift Supervision, Treasury; and the National Credit Union Administration. The final rules are available in the Federal Register. See Department of the Treasury, Office of the Comptroller of the Currency; Federal Reserve System; Federal Deposit Insurance Corporation; Department of the Treasury, Office of Thrift Supervision; National Credit Union Administration; Federal Trade Commission, "Identity Theft Red Flags and Address Discrepancies Under the Fair and Accurate Credit Transactions Act of 2003; Final Rule," 72 *Federal Register* 63718 - 63775, November 9, 2007.

[24] The FCRA is codified at 15 U.S.C. §1681.

[25] Under the Red Flags Rule, a creditor is defined as "any person who regularly extends, renews, or continues credit; any person who regularly arranges for the extension, renewal, or continuation of credit; or any assignee of an original creditor who participates in the decision to extend, renew, or continue credit," 15 U.S.C. §1691a. The Red Flag Program Clarification Act of 2010 (S. 3987), signed by President Obama on December 18, 2010, limits this definition of a creditor, excluding any creditor "that advances funds on behalf of a person for expenses incidental to a service provided by the creditor to that person."

[26] Under the Red Flags Rule, a financial institution is defined as "a State or National bank, a State or Federal savings and loan association, a mutual savings bank, a State or Federal credit union, or any other person that, directly or indirectly, holds a transaction account (as defined in §461(b) of title 12) belonging to a consumer," 15 U.S.C. §1681a(t).

[27] A covered account is one that is used primarily for personal, family, or household purposes, and that involves multiple payments or transactions. These include credit card accounts, mortgage loans, automobile loans, margin accounts, cell phone accounts, utility accounts, checking accounts, savings accounts, and other accounts for which there is a foreseeable risk of identity theft. The Rule also requires creditors and financial institutions to periodically determine whether they maintain any covered accounts, 72 *Federal Register* 63719.

[28] Federal Trade Commission, "Agencies Issue Final Rules on Identity Theft Red Flags and Notices of Address Discrepancy," press release, October 31, 2007, http://ftc.gov/opa/2007/10/redflag.shtm.

[29] http://www.ftc.gov/bcp/edu/pubs/business/alerts/alt050.shtm.

[30] Federal Trade Commission, "FTC Will Grant Six-Month Delay of Enforcement of 'Red Flags' Rule Requiring Creditors and Financial Institutions to Have Identity Theft Prevention Programs," press release, October 22, 2008, http://www.ftc.gov/opa/2008/10/redflags.shtm.

[31] Federal Trade Commission, "FTC Will Grant Three-Month Delay of Enforcement of 'Red Flags' Rule Requiring Creditors and Financial Institutions to Adopt Identity Theft Prevention Programs," press release, April 30, 2009, http://www.ftc.gov/opa/2009/04/redflagsrule.shtm.

[32] Federal Trade Commission, "FTC Extends Enforcement Deadline for Identity Theft Red Flags Rule," press release, October 30, 2009, http://www.ftc.gov/opa/2009/10/redflags.shtm.

[33] Federal Trade Commission, "FTC Extends Enforcement Deadline for Identity Theft Red Flags Rule," press release, May 28, 2010, http://www.ftc.gov/opa/2010/05/redflags.shtm.

[34] The FTC has published a guide to assist businesses in creating the identity theft prevention programs, available at Federal Trade Commission, *Fighting Fraud With the Red Flags Rule: A How-To Guide for Business*, March 2009, http://www.ftc.gov/bcp/edu/pubs/business/idtheft/bus23.pdf.

[35] Identity Theft Red Flags Final Rule, p. 63741.

[36] Ibid. Cost estimates are provided by OMB in three-year increments. Therefore, cost estimates for subsequent years are unavailable and could change from the estimates provided for the first three years.

[37] Letter from American Medical Association et al. to William E. Kovacic, Chairman, U.S. Federal Trade Commission, September 30, 2008, http://www.ama-assn.org/ama1/pub/upload/mm/31/ftc_letter20080930.pdf. HIPAA was enacted by P.L. 104-191. Fore more information on HIPAA or health information privacy, see CRS Report R40546, *The Privacy and Security Provisions for Health Information in the American Recovery and Reinvestment Act of 2009*, by Gina Stevens and Edward C. Liu.

[38] Javelin Strategy & Research, *2011 Identity Fraud Survey Report: Consumer Version*, February 2011.

[39] Between 2000 and 2010, the proportion of consumer fraud complaints that are classified as identity theft complaints has ranged from about 22% to about 40%. The total number of identity theft and other fraud complaints reported to the FTC are available from the annual Identity Theft Clearinghouse Data reports available at http://www.ftc.gov/sentinel/reports/sentinel-annual-reports/sentinel-cy2010.pdf.

[40] Statistics are available on the proportion of cyber-related crimes committed by perpetrators from various countries. However, only a proportion of those crimes are identity theft crimes, and analysts therefore cannot reliably extrapolate the proportion of identity theft crimes committed by domestic and international criminals.

[41] Federal Bureau of Investigation, *Financial Crimes Report to the Public*, Fiscal Year 2006, http://www.fbi.gov/publications/financial/fcs_report2006/publicrpt06.pdf.

[42] Wade Baker et al., 2011 Data Breach Investigations Report: A Study Conducted by the Verizon RISK Team in Cooperation with the United States Secret Service and the Dutch High Tech Crime Unit, Verizon, 2011, pp. 17-20, http://www.verizonbusiness.com/resources/reports/rp_data-breach-investigations-report-2011_en_xg.pdf. Of note, external agents were involved in 92% of all data breaches.

[43] Federal Trade Commission, *Consumer Sentinel Network Data Book for January – December, 2010*, March, 2011, http://www.ftc.gov/sentinel/reports/sentinel-annual-reports/sentinel-cy2010.pdf.

[44] Graeme R. Newman and Megan M. McNally, "Identity Theft Literature Review," Prepared for presentation and discussion at the National Institute of Justice Focus Group Meeting to develop a research agenda to identify the most effective avenues of research that will impact on prevention, harm reduction and enforcement, Contract #2005-TO-008,January 2005, http://www.ncjrs.gov/pdffiles1/nij/grants/210459.pdf.

[45] U.S. Department of Justice, *Fact Sheet: The Work of the President's Identity Theft Task Force*, September 19, 2006, p. 3, http://www.ftc.gov/os/2006/09/060919IDtheftfactsheet.pdf.

[46] Federal Bureau of Investigation, *Financial Crimes Report to the Public*, Fiscal Year 2006, http://www.fbi.gov/publications/financial/fcs_report2006/publicrpt06.pdf.

[47] See the IC3 website at http://www.ic3.gov/default.aspx. Among the many Internet crimes reported to the IC3 are identity theft and phishing. Phishing refers to gathering identity information from victims under false pretences, such as pretending to be a representative of a financial institution collecting personal information to update financial records.

[48] The IC3 received a total of 303,809 Internet crime complaints. However, it did not make publically available the exact number of these complaints which were identity theft complaints, but rather indicated that identity theft made up about 9.8% of total Internet crime complaints. Internet Crime Complaint Center, *2010 Internet Crime Report*, http://www.ic3.gov/media/annualreport/2010_IC3Report.pdf.

[49] 18 U.S.C. §3056.

[50] U.S. Secret Service, *United States Secret Service, Fiscal Year 2010 Annual Report*, http://www.secretservice.gov/USSS2010AYweb.pdf.

[51] Information provided to CRS by the USSS office of Congressional Affairs.

[52] Data provided to CRS by the USPIS Office of Congressional Affairs, November 30, 2011.

[53] U.S. Postal Inspection Service, *U.S. Postal Inspection Service Annual Report FY2010*, http://www.postalinspectorsvideo.com/uspis/AnnualReport2010.pdf.

[54] United States Postal Inspection Service, *FY2007 Annual Report of Investigations of the United States Postal Inspection Service*, January 2008, pp. 16-17, https://postalinspectors.uspis.gov/radDocs/pubs/AR2007.pdf.

[55] Social Security Administration, *Identity Theft Fact Sheet*, October 2006, http://www.socialsecurity.gov/pubs/idtheft.htm.

[56] Information provided to CRS by the Social Security Administration, Office of the Inspector General, Office of Congressional Affairs, March 25, 2009.

[57] U.S. Immigration and Customs Enforcement, *ICE Fiscal Year 2008 Annual Report: Protecting National Security and Upholding Public Safety*, 2008, p. iv, http://www.ice.gov/doclib/pi/reports/ice_annual_report/pdf/ice08ar_final.pdf.

[58] There may be multiple defendants in a case. Of note, **Figure 3** depicts the number of defendants (rather than the number of cases) prosecuted and convicted on charges of identity theft and aggravated identity theft for FY1998 through FY2010.

[59] Javelin Strategy & Research, "Javelin Study Finds Identity Fraud Reached New High in 2009, but Consumers are Fighting Back," press release, February 10, 2010, https://www.javelinstrategy.com/news/831/92/Javelin-Study-Finds-Identity-Fraud-Reached-New-High-in-2009-but-Consumers-are-Fighting-Back/d,pressRoomDetail.

[60] Javelin Strategy & Research, *2011 Identity Fraud Survey Report: Consumer Version*, February 2011.

[61] Federal Trade Commission, *Prepared Statement of the Federal Trade Commission Before the Subcommittee on Crime, Terrorism, and Homeland Security, House Committee on the Judiciary, on Protecting Consumer Privacy and Combating Identity Theft*, Washington, DC, December 18, 2007, p. 2, http://www.ftc.gov/os/testimony/P065404idtheft.pdf.

[62] Although there are estimates regarding the cost of identity theft to consumers, CRS was unable to locate any comprehensive, reliable data on the costs of identity theft (separate from the total cost of financial fraud) to the credit card industry.

[63] Federal Trade Commission, *Consumer Sentinel Network Data Book for January–December, 2010*, March, 2011, http://www.ftc.gov/sentinel/reports/sentinel-annual-reports/sentinel-cy2010.pdf.

[64] Ibid.

[65] Credit card fraud is codified at 18 U.S.C. §1029.

[66] Identity Theft Resource Center, *ITRC Forecasts Black Ice Ahead in 2011*, December 15, 2010, http://www.idtheftcenter.org/artman2/publish/m_press/ITRC_Forecasts_for_2011.shtml.

[67] Federal Bureau of Investigation, *Operation Power Outage: Armenian Organized Crime Group Targeted*, April 3, 2011, http://www.fbi.gov/news/stories/2011/march/armenian_030311/armenian_030311.

[68] Document fraud is codified at 18 U.S.C. §1028. The statutory definition of identity theft is found within this section of the Code at 18 U.S.C. §1028(a)(7).

[69] A complete discussion of immigration-related document fraud is outside the scope of this chapter, but more information can be found in CRS Report RL34007, *Immigration Fraud: Policies, Investigations, and Issues*, by Ruth Ellen Wasem.

[70] Department of Justice, *Transcript of Attorney General Remarks at Identity Theft Press Conference Held With FTC Trade Commission Chairman Timothy J. Muris and Senator Diane Feinstein*, DOJ Conference Center, May 2, 2002, http://www.usdoj.gov/archive/ag/speeches/2002/050202agidthefttranscript.htm. Also cited in U.S. General Accounting Office, *Identity Fraud: Prevalence and Links to Alien Illegal Activities*, GAO-02-830T, June 25, 2002, p. 9, http://www.gao.gov/new.items/d02830t.pdf.

[71] Federal Bureau of Investigation, "More Than Two Dozen Identified in Massive Fraudulent Document Manufacturing Operation in Los Angeles," press release, November 3, 2011,

http://www.fbi.gov/losangeles/press-releases/2011/more-than-two-dozen-identified-in-massive-fraudulent-document-manufacturing-operation-in-los-angeles.

[72] According to the Bureau of Labor Statistics (BLS), the unemployment rate has remained at or above 9.0% since May 2009, http://data.bls.gov/timeseries/LNS14000000.

[73] Identity Theft Resource Center, *2010 Breach Stats*, December 29, 2010, http://www.idtheftcenter.org/ITRC%20Breach%20Stats%20Report%202010.pdf. The IRTC indicates that the criteria for qualifying as a data breach is "[a]ny name or number that may be used, alone or in conjunction with other information, to identify a specific individual, including: name, Social Security number, date of birth. Banking or financial account number, credit card or debit card number with or without a PIN, official state or government issued driver's license or identification number, passport identification number, alien registration number, employer or taxpayer identification number, or insurance policy or subscriber numbers; unique biometric data; [or] electronic identification number, address or routing code or telecommunication identifying information or device."

[74] The Cybersecurity Act of 2012 (S. 2105) would, among other things, require the Secretary of Homeland Security and the Secretary of Defense to submit reports to Congress that would include information on cyber incidents involving Executive branch agency networks and Defense networks, respectively. These reports would contain information such as the number of breaches, data compromised, and costs to remedy the breaches.

[75] For more information on data breach notification laws affecting the private and public sectors, see CRS Report RL34120, *Federal Information Security and Data Breach Notification Laws*, by Gina Stevens.

[76] National Conference of State Legislatures, *State Security Breach Notification Laws*, http://www.ncsl.org/programs/lis/cip/priv/breachlaws.htm.

[77] CRS calculated this figure from the data provided from the Identity Theft Resource Center, *2010 Breach Stats*, December 29, 2010, http://www.idtheftcenter.org/ITRC%20Breach%20Stats%20Report%202010.pdf.

[78] Findings from Javelin Strategy & Research cited in Ben Worthen, "Cardholders Buy Peace of Mind, If Not Security," *The Wall Street Journal*, March 10, 2009, p. D1.

[79] Javelin Strategy & Research, *2011 Identity Fraud Survey Report: Consumer Version*, February 2011.

[80] Rachel Kim, *2009 Identity Fraud Survey Report: Consumer Version*, Javelin Strategy & Research, February 2009,http://www.javelinstrategy.com.

[81] Synovate, *Federal Trade Commission: 2006 Identity Theft Survey Report*, November 2007, http://www.ftc.gov/os/2007/11/SynovateFinalReportIDTheft2006.pdf.

[82] Gary R. Gordon, Donald J. Rebovich, and Kyung-Seok Choo, et al., *Identity Fraud Trends and Patterns: Building a Data-Based Foundation for Proactive Enforcement*, Center for Identity Management and Information Protection, Utica College, OJP, BJA Grant No. 2006-DD-BX-K086, October 2007, http://www.utica.edu/academic/institutes/ecii/publications/media/cimip_id_theft_study_oct_22_noon.pdf.

[83] For example, the Veterans Affairs Information Security Act, Title IX of P.L. 109-461 requires the Veterans Administration (VA) to implement an information security program to protect its sensitive personal information. For more information, see CRS Report RL34120, *Federal Information Security and Data Breach Notification Laws*, by Gina Stevens. Also, the Health Information Technology for Economic and Clinical Health (HITECH) Act, in P.L. 111-5, established—among other things—a notification requirement for a breach of non-encrypted health information. For further information on the HITECH Act, see CRS Report R40161, *The Health Information Technology for Economic and Clinical Health (HITECH) Act*, by C. Stephen Redhead.

[84] The President's Identity Theft Task Force, *Combating Identity Theft: A Strategic Plan*, April 23, 2007, http://www.identitytheft.gov/reports/StrategicPlan.pdf.

[85] For a complete discussion of the collection, disclosure, and confidentiality of Social Security numbers, see CRS Report RL30318, *The Social Security Number: Legal Developments Affecting Its Collection, Disclosure, and Confidentiality*, by Kathleen S. Swendiman.

[86] U.S. Government Accountability Office, *Social Security Numbers: Use is Widespread and Protection Could be Improved*, GAO-07-1023T, June 21, 2007, http://www.gao.gov/new.items/d071023t.pdf.

[87] Social Security Administration, Office of the Inspector General, *Removing Social Security Numbers From Medicare Cards*, A-08-08-18026, May 2008, p. 1, http://www.ssa.gov/oig/ADOBEPDF/A-08-08-18026.pdf.

[88] Ibid., p. 3.

[89] 42 U.S.C. §13925.

[90] U.S. Government Accountability Office, *Social Security Numbers: Use is Widespread and Protection Could be Improved*, GAO-07-1023T, June 21, 2007, pp. 12-13, http://www.gao.gov/new.items/d071023t.pdf.

[91] Ibid.

[92] See, for example, Alessandro Acquisti and Ralph Gross, "Social Insecurity: The Unintended Consequences of Identity Fraud Prevention Policies," http://www.heinz.cmu.edu/~acquisti/papers/acquisti-MISQ.pdf.

[93] Ibid.

[94] Synovate, *Federal Trade Commission: 2006 Identity Theft Survey Report*, November 2007, http://www.ftc.gov/os/2007/11/SynovateFinalReportIDTheft2006.pdf.

[95] Gary R. Gordon, Donald J. Rebovich, and Kyung-Seok Choo, et al., *Identity Fraud Trends and Patterns: Building a Data-Based Foundation for Proactive Enforcement*, Center for Identity Management and Information Protection, Utica College, OJP, BJA Grant No. 2006-DD-BX-K086, October 2007, http://www.utica.edu/academic/institutes/ecii/publications/media/cimip_id_theft_study_oct_22_noon.pdf.

[96] Javelin Strategy & Research, "Latest Javelin Research Shows Identity Fraud Increased 22 Percent, Affecting Nearly Ten Million Americans: But Consumer Costs Fell Sharply by 31 Percent," press release, February 9, 2009, http://www.javelinstrategy.com/2009/02/09/latest-javelin-research-shows-identity-fraud-increased-22-percent-affecting-nearly-ten-million-americans-but-consumer-costs-fell-sharply-by-31-percent/.

[97] Sasha Romanosky, Rahul Telang, and Alessandro Acquisti, "Do Data Breach Disclosure Laws Reduce Identity Theft?," Seventh Workshop on the Economics of Information Security, Center for Digital Strategies, Tuck School of Business, Dartmouth College, Hanover, NH, June 25, 2008, http://weis2008.econinfosec.org/papers/Romanosky.pdf.

[98] Findings from Javelin Strategy & Research cited in Ben Worthen, "Cardholders Buy Peace of Mind, If Not Security," *The Wall Street Journal*, March 10, 2009, p. D1.

[99] A complete discussion of relevant cyber security issues is outside the scope of this chapter. However, see CRS Report R40427, *Comprehensive National Cybersecurity Initiative: Legal Authorities and Policy Considerations*, by John Rollins and Anna C. Henning for a discussion of current issues in cyber security.

[100] The President's Identity Theft Task Force, *Combating Identity Theft: A Strategic Plan*, April 23, 2007, at http://www.identitytheft.gov/reports/StrategicPlan.pdf.

[101] 18 U.S.C. §1708.

[102] 18 U.S.C. §513.

[103] 26 U.S.C. §7201, 7206-7207.

[104] The President's Identity Theft Task Force, *Combating Identity Theft: A Strategic Plan*, April 23, 2007, pp. 91-92, at http://www.identitytheft.gov/reports/StrategicPlan.pdf.

[105] See the Seniors' Identity Protection Act of 2011 (H.R. 978), the Medicare Identity Theft Prevention Act of 2011 (H.R. 1509), and the Social Security Number Protection Act of 2011 (S. 1275).

[106] See the Social Security Child Protection Act of 2011 (H.R. 3008).

[107] See the Tax Crimes and Identity Theft Prevention Act (H.R. 3482) and the Identify [sic] Theft and Tax Fraud Prevention Act (H.R. 3215, S. 1534).

[108] See, for example, the Protecting the Privacy of Social Security Numbers Act (S. 1199).

[109] See H.R. 1538, the Social Security Identity Defense Act of 2011.

[110] See the Data Accountability and Trust Act (H.R. 1707), the Data Accountability and Trust Act (DATA) of 2011 (H.R. 1841), the SAFE Data Act (H.R. 2577), the Personal Data Privacy and Security Act of 2011 (S. 1151), the Data Security and Breach Notification Act of 2011 (S. 1207), the Data Breach Notification Act of 2011 (S. 1408), and the Personal Data Protection and Breach Accountability Act of 2011 (S. 1535).

INDEX

D

E

F

G